WHAT *THE EXORCIST* DIDN'T TELL YOU, THIS BOOK WILL—

Learn how to use your spiritual authority as Pat Brooks gives you practical advice and examples of deliverance, including prayers of renunciation of the occult, prayers for forgiveness, and helpful Scriptures that will enable you to ward off satanic attacks.

Using Your Spiritual Authority

Pat Brooks

Introduction by Don Basham

Banner Publishing
504 LAUREL DRIVE
MONROEVILLE, PENNSYLVANIA 15146

Scripture references are
from the New American Standard Bible,
except for a few familiar phrases
from the King James Bible.

© 1973 by Whitaker House
Printed in the United States of America

ISBN 0-88368-023-8

Banner Publishing
504 Laurel Drive
Monroeville, Pennsylvania 15146
(412) 372-6420

This book is dedicated to
the Lord Jesus Christ,
the
DELIVERER

Introduction

It is no secret that the Church of Jesus Christ is in the midst of spiritual renewal. Miracles of healing, the baptism in the Holy Spirit, deliverance from demonic powers, along with other manifestations of spiritual gifts are on the increase throughout the Body of Christ. Ministries proclaiming this dimension of God's activity seem singularly anointed by the Holy Spirit.

Significantly, the Spirit blesses both ministry and message. Some Christian books published today obviously have a unique spiritual anointing upon them. I believe Pat Brooks' *Using Your Spiritual Authority* is one of those books. The quiet confidence which pervades its clear teaching is eloquent testimony to the spiritual authority of which it speaks.

Deep biblical insight and practical instruction backed by personal experience combine to offer new spiritual victory to every believer. My own life has been strengthened and my own convictions deepened by reading this book. And as I read, I found myself thanking God for the many who will be released from Satan's snare by wielding the spiritual authority made real to them through these pages.

> Don W. Basham
> Author of
> *Face Up With A Miracle*
> and *Deliver Us From Evil*

Contents

1. Belonging to the Lord Jesus Christ: Source of Authority 11
2. Obeying the First Commandments 25
3. Submitting to Earthly Authority 37
4. Binding the Spirits 47
5. Discerning of Spirits 59
6. Casting Out Spirits 73
7. Wrestling Against Rulers 91
8. Keeping Your Deliverance 103

1 | Belonging to the Lord Jesus Christ: Source of Authority

As a little girl growing up in the Shenendoah Valley I had certain privileges which city children frequently miss. There were the long walks up the hill behind our house and the hours spent lying on the soft meadow grass. Sometimes the gentle caress of a soft breeze on my cheeks, as I lay there under the Dresden china blue sky, seemed to bring an answer from the One for whom I reached so often.

Reminiscing about those precious days now, I realize they were mine because I belonged to my family. My father happened to work near Roanoke, Virginia, and, as one of his children, I was entitled to the sheer joy of this environment because it was where we lived. There was no way I could have provided this happy setting for myself; it was simply my right as one of my father's children.

In much the same way, God longs for His own to bask in His presence and enjoy the fresh, pure breath of His Spirit in their lives—to enjoy all He has provided for them—just because they are in His family! How it must grieve Him to see His children groping about in the cellars of their lives, inhaling the foul stench of satanic deception, when they could be out in the fresh air—

11

rejoicing in His truth, led by His Spirit, and bathed in His love.

Once Jesus said to His followers, "If you abide in My word, then you are truly disciples of Mine; and you shall know the truth, and the truth shall make you free" (John 8:31, 32). The Bible is God's great map to lead us out of any swamp or wasteland in which we find ourselves. The Spirit of Truth will faithfully blow open any cellar door we have allowed to close behind us and beckon us to the fresh air and sunshine of the "life hidden with Christ in God" (Col. 3:3).

Over the years my husband has patiently given me several good lessons on the fine art of map reading. (Like many women, I find maps and time tables equally bewildering and complex, especially since one is almost always in a hurry when they are needed!) Finally, Dick introduced me to a revolutionary concept which cleared much of my confusion on this subject: *a map will only help you if you know where you are!*

Every person born into this world has to find his starting point on God's map if he is ever to discover the promised land of blessing. Everyone must admit to himself where he is. He is at the spot Bunyan called "the City of Destruction," and all who stay there are lost. There is only one way out of this place, and that way is Jesus Christ. Unlike founders of other religions, Jesus never promised to *show* people the way to God. Instead, he stated simply, "I am the way, and the truth, and the life; no one comes to the Father, but through Me" (John 14:6).

When morally upright, religious Nicodemus

came to Jesus one night because of a longing to be sure of his standing with God, the Lord told him plainly that he must be born again. When Nicodemus asked if this rebirth were physical, Jesus firmly assured him otherwise. A beginning of spiritual life was as necessary to sophisticated Nicodemus as a beginning of physical life had been. Physical birth had put him on the road of earthly life; spiritual rebirth would set him on the road of eternal life.

The Spirit of God brings about this new birth. Jesus compared the Spirit's work to the work of nature's wind. We can never see the wind itself, but always see the results of it in the trees, clouds, water and so on. In much the same way, although we do not see the Holy Spirit implanting divine life into a human spirit, we see some of its results in the transformation of character which follows. "Therefore if any man is in Christ, he is a new creature; the old things passed away; behold, new things have come" (2 Cor. 5:17).

When Nicodemus was faced with this startling fact, he wanted to know how such a strange miracle could take place. Jesus answered by referring to this incident in the history of Israel's wilderness wanderings.

"Then they set out from Mount Hor by the way of the Red Sea, to go around the land of Edom; and the people became impatient because of the journey. And the people spoke against God and Moses, 'Why have you brought us out of Egypt to die in the wilderness? For there is no food and no water, and we loathe this miserable food.' And the Lord sent fiery serpents among the people and they bit the people, so that many people of Israel died. So the people came to Moses and said, 'We have sinned, because we have spoken against the Lord and you; intercede with the Lord, that He may remove the serpents from us.' And Moses interceded for the people. Then the Lord said to Moses, 'Make a fiery serpent, and set it on a standard; and it shall come about, that everyone who is bitten, when he looks at it, he shall live.' And Moses made a bronze serpent and set it on the standard; and it came about, that if a serpent bit any man, when he looked to the bronze serpent, he lived" (Numbers 21:4-9).

It is not hard to picture the bedlam in a camp of two million people, many of whom have been bitten by deadly snakes. There must have been two types of reaction to Moses' news of God's cure. A brief excursion into the imagination will serve to bring them into focus.

Let us assume that "Benammi" and "David" have both been bitten by the snakes. Writhing in their tents and with ominous swelling in their limbs, each hears a runner going through the camp with this news: "God has told Moses the cure for these snake bites. Just get someone to bring you out to the plain where Moses has a brass serpent in a pole. Look at it, and you will live!"

Benammi's wife sends for a stretcher, but he curses and yells at her. "Forget it, woman!" he screams. "What I need is some antivenin, and here some idiot is blabbering about looking at a brass snake on a pole! Get out of here and get me some real help! What do you think I am—a fool?"

In the tent next door, David's wife sends for a stretcher and two men to carry it. David says in wonder, "Well, I don't see how looking at a brass snake hanging on a pole would really save my life, but if God says so, I'll do it."

Without a second's hesitation we may flatly state that Benammi died, but David lived. Why? Because God's Word says so. All who obeyed lived. David chose the way of escape from death and destruction. God had provided that way to anyone who would take a simple look of faith. Benammi died in his unbelief.

Just as the dying Israelite had no hope of life apart from God's remedy, so each of us must face the truth that we are spiritually dead until we take that look of faith at Jesus Christ on the cross, where He died to suffer the penalty for our sins. In fact, the bronze serpent is merely Second Corinthians 5:21 in picture form: "He made Him who knew no sin to be sin on our behalf, that we might become the righteousness of God in Him."

Sometime ago I had the privilege of sharing this graphic, scriptural confrontation with a young couple whose hearts the Lord had prepared. Just as I always do at this point in the story, I asked this man and wife if they understood what it meant to take the look of faith—and if they felt ready to take such a step themselves. Without any hesitation, they both said they did understand and were ready to receive Christ as Savior and Lord.

Then Carole told her husband and me this amazing story. Eleven years before she had gone to a Billy Graham crusade and had felt just the same way (i.e., that she should make a decision for Christ). However, her date that night had been mocking the entire meeting, and she was afraid he would laugh at her if she went forward. Therefore she decided to wait until the next morning to commit her life to Christ, but try as she might, she could not believe the same way the next day! Burying her face in her hands, she confessed, "I've never felt that way again until tonight—never understood it again clearly until now. I'd never let this opportunity slip by without coming to Christ."

The joy in that home that night can be yours right there where you are reading, if you understand the issue as clearly as that young couple did and commit your life to Christ at this moment. Don't depend on seeing it clearly some other time. The Bible says, "Now is the day of salvation" (2 Cor. 6:2). Who really knows if he will have tomorrow, anyway? The moment we get light from God is the time to walk in it. If you have never before said that final, eternal "yes" to Jesus Christ, just bow your head and say something like this to Him: "Lord, I know I'm a sinner, and there's not a thing I ever tried which really changed me completely on the inside. Thank you for dying for my sin. Now I invite you to come into my life and live out your resurrection life through me, cleansing me from my fatal snake bite of sin with your precious Blood."

It was no accident that God used snakes to punish His people for their sin. In the garden of Eden, Eve (whom Scripture calls the mother of all living), passed on her spiritual mutation to the whole human race when she doubted God's Word and believed the serpent's lie. Since then humanity has been bitten with the fatal snake bite of sin, for which God Himself has the only cure.

The Lord's perfect righteousness demanded the death penalty for sin, but His perfect love made Him leave the judge's bench and come down to us in Christ to suffer it for our sakes. Hebrews 9:22 says, "Without shedding of blood there is no forgiveness." John the Baptist understood this mystery when he recognized Jesus as the "Lamb of God who takes away the sin of the world!" (John 1:29). All the unblemished lambs slain on Old Testament altars were but types and shadows of the sinless, peerless Lamb who shed His blood for the sin of everyone in the world who will believe Him.

Once we see this by faith, we put away forever any notion that we can save ourselves. All we can do is humbly thank the Lord Jesus Christ for conquering sin and death on Calvary and having proved His victory by being raised from the dead. We repent—turn back from the road we have been traveling which leads to death and hell—and start going in the exact opposite direction toward eternal life and heaven. Such a change causes, first of all, a profoundly different attitude. The things we once loved we hate; the things we once hated we love. Some people and places have now vanished from our lives, for they are still part of that city we have left, and they have no desire to follow us. Yet on this new road there are amazing landmarks and precious people with whom to share them. Our new lives are not empty, but fuller than we ever dreamed possible while we were still dead on the inside.

My home sits just a few hundred yards from the Adirondack Northway—a superhighway to Montreal from the New York Thruway. In the summer traffic is heavy, not only with cars bound for Canada, but also with those headed for the lovely lakes to the north. People take this road because it is the safest, fastest, best route to their destination, as any map will clearly show.

In much the same way, Scripture points out a highway to those who have been born into the family of God by faith in Christ Jesus. Trying other roads invites delays at best and disaster at worst. Therefore it behooves us to find this excellent road early in our journey and travel on it for the rest of our lives. The prophet Isaiah called it "the highway of holiness," whereas the apostle Paul pointed it out as the way of the exchanged life. He summarized it in Galatians 2:20. "I have been crucified with Christ; and it is no longer I who live, but Christ lives in me; and the life which I now live in the flesh I live by faith in the Son of God, who loved me, and delivered Himself up for me."

The detailed portions of the map showing this magnificent highway are in Romans 6 through 8 and Ephesians 1 and 2. Here God's wonderful plan for complete victory in the Christian life is laid out with great precision. Briefly summarized, it is a call to the believer to understand that he can never live a life pleasing to God and must therefore cease all fruitless efforts to do so. Rather, he must recognize that only Jesus Christ ever could, did, or shall live a life pleasing to God. Since we are joined to Him forever by faith, we are to *know* the old man (our natural, fleshly life) died on the cross with Him, and count on that fact for the rest of our earthly lives. As our old self died in Him, so the Holy Spirit brings new life. We are raised with Him from the dead and seated "in the heavenly places in Christ Jesus" (Eph 2:6).

In other words, because I am *in Christ*, His authority is mine to use here on earth. His Holy Spirit makes available to each believer the power to use His authority. We may receive this power by asking Him in faith for the baptism in the Holy Spirit.

Shall I be a pauper or a millionaire in my spiritual life? It is mine to decide. If I trust the Holy Spirit to empower me, I can live a life in union with my crucified, risen, ascended Lord. Whether I see and act upon this truth will determine whether I walk in victory or not.

There are millions of believers today who have no trouble accepting the fact that they are one with Christ in his death, burial, and resurrection (Romans 6 through 8). Yet very few realize that they are also one with Him in His ascension and present position of authority over the unseen world seated at the right hand of God. The apostle Paul knew that to experience this truth required special revelation from God, for he requested such light for his readers in his earnest, magnificent prayer of Ephesians 1:15-23.

The Lord Jesus Christ defeated Satan completely by His atoning death on Calvary, but ever since then, the demon world has made it their prime task to keep the church from discovering this fact. Much current preaching emphasizes that a believer has all he will ever need at conversion, the moment of rebirth. Unfortunately, such teaching fails to show that all we ever get from God is what we appropriate by faith. We must actively trust God for all that is ours by inheritance, or it can not become ours in experience. John 1:12 says, "But as many as received Him, to them He gave the right to become children of God, even to those who believe in His name:"

A "right" implies the potential for ownership. After a person has died and his estate has been settled, all heirs mentioned in the will have a right to their inheritance. However, some banks have sizable unclaimed sums waiting for heirs who have never appeared. Occasionally this strange situation may have been caused by jealous relatives who never informed the rightful heir of his inheritance.

Likewise, with sinister malice the powers of darkness have kept the children of God from knowing of their full inheritance in Christ. Cunning, deceptive spirits influence or close the minds of believers with arguments designed to keep them from ever writing on God's blank checks. The inexhaustible supply of power, authority and joy deposited in their names by Jesus Christ is unknown to thousands. Thus, many die as spiritual paupers after living a lifetime unaware of the fortune which was theirs for the claiming. It is God's will for His children to live powerful, radiant, joyful lives characterized by vibrant physical, mental, and spiritual health. Yet how many never find such victory, simply because they did not know they were entitled to it.

Christians are often polite, humble people. They would not dream of being forward or "pushy" with God. Frequently they accept repeated physical complaints, depression, anxiety, or a host of other torments because they piously assume these to be the will of God for their lives. How surprised they are to find that the Lord never intended such things for His children and is even grieved when they attribute such plans to Him!

In the very beginning of His earthly ministry, the Lord Jesus Christ appointed disciples "that they might be with Him, and that He might send them out to preach, and to have authority to cast out the demons" (Mark 3:14 & 15). It was evidently the intent of the Lord that the preaching of the gospel be accompanied by the deliverance ministry, and such was the practice of those early believers. In Luke 10 we find that the seventy were amazed that the demons were subject to them in Jesus' name. In Acts 8 we read of evangelism coupled with the casting out of demons and healing of the sick under the ministry of Philip the deacon. The apostle Paul cast a demon out of a girl following him in Acts 16.

From these widely divergent passages, we can see that the ministries of power were the norm, rather than the exception, for the early church. And so they were meant to be!

"And these signs will accompany those who have believed: in My name they will cast out demons, they will speak with new tongues; they will pick up serpents, and if they drink any deadly poison, it shall not hurt them; they will lay hands on the sick and they will recover." (Mark 16: 17 & 18)

Although this passage of Scripture has been controversial for some, history has documented cases of such occurrences scattered over the past two thousand years. St. Augustine wrote that it was to be expected that believers would speak with new tongues, and occasional references to healings and exorcism are also found throughout the ages.

In the present outpouring of the Holy Spirit, the church is again being empowered to take the good news to the whole man. Where believers are taking Jesus Christ at His Word today, they are having New Testament experiences and results. In contemporary Indonesia almost every miracle of the Bible has been repeated many times, as those with childlike faith trust God to work on their behalf as they evangelize their land. Raisings from the dead, multitudes of healings and deliverances, walking on the water, seeing water changed into wine for communion—all these have been experienced by the Indonesian church on the island of Timor. (*Like A Mighty Wind*, by Mel Tari, Creation House, 1970.) In the wake of this undeniable evidence of the power of God, multitudes of Muslims have forsaken the way of their fathers and have put their trust in Jesus Christ.

In recent years North and South America have also been experiencing increasing revival. Miracles of healing and deliverance are happening here in the western world as God awakens His sleeping giant, the church or body of Christ.

Not only have lengthening of limbs, healings, and deliverances become common in some groups, but also there are occasional reports of even more extraordinary miracles. Babs and Bill Owen of Easton, Maryland, friends of the author, told us of speaking with a humble pastor in Mexico who went with his elders to pray for a twelve year old girl. She was a daughter of one of the elders and had been murdered by enemies of the gospel. A bullet had entered her head from the front and come out of the back of her neck. As the men laid hands on her and prayed, they saw the holes close up and the flesh restored to normal. Little pieces of neck bone chips were forced out onto the pillow as the miracle took place. The child awoke to live again by the mighty power of the name of Jesus Christ.

It is about time that the church of Jesus Christ act as His body and take His glorious salvation to a lost and dying world on His terms, not ours. Of course, it is good news that Christ died for our sins. However, it is even better news to find out that He took all that we are and nailed it to His cross, raising us with Him to a new kind of life in His resurrection. In Him we are also seated in the position of authority at the right hand of the Father, and all His and our enemies have been put under our feet (Psalm 8:6; I Corinthians 15:27; Ephesians 1:22; 2:6).

No wonder He said, "Behold, I have given you authority to tread upon serpents and scorpions, and over all the power of the enemy, and nothing shall injure you." (Luke 10:19)

2 | Obeying the First Commandments

A brother in Christ with a practical, no-nonsense approach to his faith prayed this way: "Lord Jesus, thank you for making me miserable until I went and talked to that man as you told me to. I'm glad you're the Boss and everything's fine between us when I do what you say."

How much misery could be spared a multitude of God's people if they only understood this!

Everywhere Jesus Christ preached, He stressed the need for people to repent and believe the gospel. Not long ago we had a vivid illustration in our New Testament Fellowship of what it meant to repent. A mightily-anointed, yet childlike brother, got up in front of the adults and children present and began walking in one direction. Then he said, "Now I repent." He turned around, and began to walk in the opposite direction.

Nothing less than this total change of direction and attitude is Biblical salvation, and we do no kindness to people if we try to convince them otherwise. Surely no tragedy will equal the plight of those at the final judgment who sincerely believed they were right with God—but who were sincerely wrong.

Jesus did not die on the Cross that we might remain exactly what we have always been and continue in the behavior that drove the nails into His flesh. Rather, He offered His blood for our sins so that He might have the opportunity to live His own life through us and to show those around us what a profound and total change this transaction can make in a life.

The first two of the ten commandments make it clear that God intends to be absolute Lord of our lives, the object of all our worship and the motivation for all our service. Yet no sin is so universal to humanity as idolatry. In the Western Hemisphere, hedonism, intellectualism, politics and human relationships often crowd God out of first place in our lives. With proper teaching, committed Christians can generally see that these things are wrong when they dominate the life. However, there is a far more dangerous form of idolatry which some believers take quite lightly. It is the threat of occultism.

Currently, popular occult practices such as fortune telling and astrology in the civilized world have their counterparts in the animism (i.e., worship of evil spirits) of primitive societies. Approximately one-third of the earth's population are animists in religious practice, a fact which archaeologists, anthropologists and historians note with equal surprise. In other words, where areas have been affected little by modern communication or evangelism, demon worship is almost universal.

Whatever our reaction to such facts as these, certain deductions seem to suggest themselves. First of all, there *are* evil powers which in some way convey their existence to human beings and hold them in fear. Second, these demons are seeking worship and pose as gods to their uninformed, sadly duped victims.

Even where a society is fairly sophisticated, it can be fully pagan. When the apostle Paul preached the gospel in Ephesus, God performed some extraordinary miracles through him. Many who had been practicing magic in that area became convinced of the superiority of God's power. They brought their books on occult involvement and built a large bonfire. Scripture records the amount of their economic loss as fifty thousand pieces of silver (Acts 19:19). Obviously the Greek-speaking world of that day must have been on a psychic binge similar to that of our own society, but with one tragic difference. First-century Christians realized that God would not tolerate occult involvement in their lives, but modern Christians are sometimes impudently blasé on the subject.

Sad to say, there are few contemporary bonfires of occult literature and games. Some have occurred in New Guinea and Indonesia in recent years. Both areas have been experiencing a mighty spiritual awakening. Recently some Jesus people in California burned occult objects worth $3,000. Also, many individual Christians are being convicted of the sin of playing with Satan's toys. Our fire place is often the scene of a ouija board or occult book going up in smoke!

A woman came to us who had become deeply involved in the occult. We explained to her from the scriptures that there would have to be a complete break with her occult practices before deliverance. We told her to burn any occult books she might have, as well as her ouija board.

She believed the word of God as it was explained to her. The following Saturday she and her two sons put the books and their ouija board into a small incinerator at the door of their garage. When the ouija board caught fire, a flame leaped several feet from the incinerator, appearing to run across the floor of the garage. An apparition of a woman's face appeared in the flame, and all three heard it scream, "You'll burn in hell for this!"

A few days after this shattering experience, this woman came for deliverance from evil spirits. A local pastor, his wife, and I worked with her for an entire afternoon. Many demons were cast out of her during that period, each one putting up a battle of some minutes before it would come out. Sometimes the demons would throw her against the side of the pew or onto the floor before they came out with loud screams.

As occasionally happens during a deliverance session, the evil spirits in this woman spoke right out of her, using her own mouth. Several demons she had were connected with religious deception. One demon, in a loud, shrieking voice began to chant the following phrase: "No love, no love, no love. Separate yourself! Separate yourself! Separate yourself!"

It is my firm conviction that this woman could never have been delivered from her torment had she not burned her occult books and objects.

If we as a nation are ever to experience the sweeping, widespread fire of revival, there will have to be some bonfires. There must also be some fires burning in the hearts of a multitude of God's people. God has not changed His mind about the occult, and He is calling for mighty repentance and a final parting with it on the part of His Church. His word to Israel on this subject is still relevant for us today:

> "When you enter the land which the Lord your God gives you, you shall not learn to imitate the detestable things of those nations. There shall not be found among you anyone who makes his son or his daughter pass through the fire, one who uses divination, one who practices witchcraft, or one who interprets omens, or a sorcerer, or one who casts a spell, or a medium, or a spiritist, or one who calls up the dead. For whoever does these things is detestable to the Lord; and because of these detestable things the Lord your God will drive them out before you. You shall be blameless before the Lord your God. For those nations which you shall dispossess, listen to those who practice witchcraft and to diviners, but as for you, the Lord your God has not allowed you to do so" (Deut. 18:9-14).

Ignorance or indifference to this warning has reaped a terrifying whirlwind throughout the world. Billy Graham says that in Great Britain 80% of the population are in some way involved with the occult, whereas only two per cent attend church. Brazil has 150 spiritist newspapers, and seances are conducted in so-called Christian services of worship. There are purported to be thousands of witches in New York City, and the hippie sub-culture of the United States is as ensnared in occult practice as it is characterized by drug usage.

In fact, one troubled young man confided to my husband and me, "Astrology is where it's at these days; that's where the big kicks are." This boy was so controlled by strange powers that he was able to look at a person and know under what sign of the zodiac he had been born. Happily, this is no longer the case, for the Lord Jesus Christ has delivered the youth from his torment. He is now a vital, witnessing Christian.

The Bible says in Isaiah 47:13 that the Lord challenged "the astrologers, the stargazers, the monthly prognosticators (horoscope readers)" to save Babylon from His curse, for its ruin and doom were certain. Genesis 11 records the probable beginning of this occult practice, for the tower of Babel was not a naive and ridiculous attempt of man to reach toward heaven in a physical sense. Instead, it was an attempt to search out the heavens in the same way that modern astrologers do. The meaning of the word translated "tower" in Genesis 11:4 is "ziggurat," a tower on whose top was a zodiac. Since this was the forerunner of the modern horoscope, it is doubly significant that God came down and confounded man's first attempt to satisfy his curiosity by occult means.

Fortunetelling, extrasensory perception, healing services characterized by metaphysical practice, addiction to drugs, water dowsing, parlor games involving levitation and body lifting, as well as the rise of religious cults, are all earmarks of the vast occult explosion of our day. In all of these activities supernatural powers are being evoked who are happy to oblige the seeker with some information to satisfy his wrong curiosity, but God detests and condemns such behavior.

God's Word continues to say some significant

things about such seeking for supernatural experience from the wrong source:

"And when they say to you, 'Consult the mediums and the wizards who whisper and mutter,' should not a people consult their God? Should they consult the dead on behalf of the living? To the law and to the testimony! If they do not speak according to this word, it is because they have no dawn" (Isaiah 8:19, 20).

"The secret things belong to the Lord our God, but the things revealed belong to us and to our sons forever, that we may observe all the words of this law" (Deut. 29:29).

"So Saul died for his trespass which he committed against the Lord, because of the word of the Lord which he did not keep; and also because he asked counsel of a medium, making inquiry of it, and did not inquire of the Lord. Therefore He killed him, and turned the kingdom to David the son of Jesse" (I Chron. 10:13, 14).

"Therefore, having these promises, beloved, let us cleanse ourselves from all defilement of flesh *and spirit*, perfecting holiness in the fear of God" (2 Cor. 7:1).

What happens if people ignore these warnings and experiment with forbidden spiritual powers? They eventually become subject to the forces with which they once played.

"For sin shall not be master over you, for you are not under law, but under grace. What then? Shall we sin because we are not under law but under grace? May it never be! Do you not know that when you present yourselves to someone as slaves for obedience, you are slaves of the one whom you obey, either of sin resulting in death, or of obedience resulting in righteousness?" (Romans 6:14-16)

Our Friday night prayer meetings have often been the scene of deliverance for those caught in a web of occult subjection, but seldom are such souls set completely free in a single evening. This fact offends some people who hasten to point out that the Lord Jesus Christ cast out the entire legion of demons from the Gadarene at once. For this argument we can only point out the following facts: the Lord Jesus Christ did a number of things during the time of His incarnation which few of us have ever seen duplicated. Also, there is virtually nothing in the account of the Gaderene's deliverance to indicate that he was seriously involved in occult practice.

In our local New Testament Fellowship we have observed that the deeper the occult involvement of the individual, the more violent and tortuous his deliverance is likely to be. Perhaps this is because God has not repealed His law of sowing and reaping, given in the Scriptures above, and aptly summarized in Galatians 6:7. "Do not be deceived, God is not mocked; for whatever a man sows, this he will also reap."

No one would suggest that Christian young people who are loose in their morals are immune to pregnancy or venereal disease. Yet many seem to think that God will wink at their occult dabbling, and they will have no torment or reaping from such deadly sowing.

A young wife and mother who came to us one Friday night has a history which vividly emphasizes the danger of occult involvement. As a teenager, Cynthia had run around with the wrong crowd, at one point dating a boy who was fascinated with witchcraft. He took her to visit a witch only once, but Cynthia cooperated with him to the extent of giving him a strand of hair that the witch used to make a charm. Many kinds of torment began in the girl's life at that point, including recurring, compulsive ideas of suicide.

Once she renounced witchcraft and any spell or curse which had been placed on her through it, Cynthia was dramatically delivered of many demons. She retched and moaned in terrible pain as each one came out, often pulling on her own hair and causing extra agony in this way. However, when they were all gone, she was wonderfully, gloriously free.

Christians and Christian groups who treat psychic dabbling lightly will begin to discover that they are increasingly unable to receive God's blessings. Several years ago a Christian youth organization published an article in its magazine suggesting that divining for water and lost objects was a harmless pastime, and even gave directions on how to make a divining rod! Since that time this group has been beset by financial need and has had to resort to many types of pleas for funds. This organization and others who encourage occult practice will continue to experience various kinds of need until open confession and repentance is made for such gross encouragement of sin in Christian youth.

God forbid that we wink at or accept what the Lord regards as an abomination!

One of the tragic harvests reaped when man sows occult seed is the passing on of some of his deepest problems and torments to succeeding generations. In the warning accompanying the first two commandments (Exodus 20:1-6) God says He visits the iniquity of the fathers on the children for three or four generations. Evidently idolatry, demon worship, and occult involvement are inseparably connected, from God's viewpoint. First Corinthians 10:20 is the climactic point in a passage warning believers to flee from idolatry and even meat sacrificed to idols.

> "No; but I say that the things which the Gentiles sacrifice they sacrifice to demons, and not to God; and I do not want you to become sharers in demons."

"Visiting iniquity" always puzzled me until we began to see people being delivered from demons. Many demons will give their names before coming out, and often these names represent specific sins or wrong attitudes, such as *pride, lust, fear, unbelief, self-pity, hate* or *rebellion*. Slowly it began to dawn upon us that unwelcome character traits often run in certain families because God literally fulfills His Word in this warning. God is always true to His Word.

There is a "payola" connected with occult involvement which no informed Christian would dare to inflict upon his family. However, many have already unwittingly harmed themselves and their loved ones with psychic experimentation. For these, it is necessary to confess each contact with the occult as sin, no matter how casual it may have been. To confess is to agree with God about the sin: to accept His view of it and turn away from it.

For many of us, muddling through life with inherited torment has become a way of life which we regard as irrevocable and which we approach with abject resignation. Praise the Lord! This need not be the case! But like all His other wonderful ways, it is by no means automatic just because we are born again. It still requires a definite act of faith and obedience on our part.

God's Word says, "If they confess their iniquity and the iniquity of their forefathers, in their unfaithfulness which they committed against Me—I also was acting in hostility against them, to bring them into the land of their enemies—or if their uncircumcised heart becomes humbled so that they make amends for their iniquity, then will I remember My covenant..." (Lev. 26:40-42).

In 1968 my husband and I were agonizing over our youngest son's problem. We could find no solution, no matter how hard we prayed. Every morning at exactly 2:45 a.m. he would cry out in terror, in the throes of horrible nightmares. His body would be stiff, his eyes glazed, and the shrieks would continue for several minutes even after he woke up and was being held in our arms.

Finally the Lord sent a friend our way who knew something of using his spiritual authority. He pointed out to us that such a weird pattern of nightmares was doubtless demonic in origin, and probably stemmed from a hereditary problem in one of our families. He led us in a simple prayer to break this psychic hold, in Jesus' Name. Although Billy was asleep upstairs as we prayed in the dining room, the demonic bondage was miraculously broken. He was never again awakened at that hour and seldom even has a bad dream.

In recent years we have known many children to be similarly delivered without being physically present, simply because their parents have taken spiritual authority in this way: "I now break, in the name of Jesus Christ, all psychic heredity, and any demonic hold upon my family line as a result of sin or disobedience in any of my ancestors!"

How wonderful to wipe out demonic torments which may have been inflicted upon our families for three or four generations in a moment of time, through the power in the matchless Name of Jesus! Should skepticism or unbelief rob us of such wonderful relief from Satan's hereditary web? How can we justify hanging on to such spiritual filth when God commands us to cleanse ourselves? (2 Corinthians 7:1).

If we are to obey fully the first commandment and have no other gods before our living Lord, we must rid our family closet of old idols which rebellious ancestors may have hidden there. Certainly we must also make a clean break with all forms of occult dabbling ourselves. When we do so, we will be conscious of a new peace and directions in our lives. We will also be freer in our great adventure with God as we get ready for the imminent return of Jesus Christ!

3 | Submitting to Earthly Authority

A mood of rebellion and anarchy is so common today that many regard respect for authority as a quaint historical phenomenon. Strikes in industry and on campus, tune-outs and sit-ins, noisy classrooms and school halls, the rising divorce rate—all point to a state of affairs where each man is doing what is right in his own eyes (Judges 21:25).

However, the whims of mankind cannot affect God's Word. He makes it clear that He is the final authority over His creation, and that He has established orderly chains of command for the accomplishment of His will here on earth. The teaching of Romans 13 is that God has ordained human government and purposes that it be obeyed. Young people who argue otherwise are usually unaware of this fact or indifferent to it. Yet ignoring truth does not change it. Wishing will not make it so, and God has some stern things to say to those who call good evil, and evil, good (Isaiah 5:20-30).

The fifth commandment (to honor one's parents) carries with it a promise of longevity and blessing. God's chain of command in the home is clearly presented in Ephesians 5. Christ is to be Head of the home, with the husband and father as human head directly under Him. Then the wife is to submit to the authority of her husband, whereas the children must be in subjection to both parents.

Larry Christenson's excellent book, *The Christian Family*,* reveals that any disruption of this divine order will result in a breakdown of the authority of that home. If the father is not submitted to Christ, he may find it difficult to command the respect of his wife and children. If the mother is not submitted to her husband, she will likely find that the children rebel at her authority over them. Children who do not submit to their parents may never develop the self-discipline and power over their own will which they need to become responsible adults.

The way out of such a vicious cycle is simply to realize that God is the Creator of all authority, and then to come under that authority in our daily lives. Submission is an act of the will. When we will to do what God says is right to do, He honors us with deep conviction in our own human spirit and gives authority and credibility to our lives as they touch others. Jesus said, "If any man is willing to do His will, he shall know the teaching, whether it is of God, or whether I speak from Myself" (John 7:17).

A careful study of the Scriptures on the subject of authority will reveal that authority is always delegated from a greater power above it, upon which it depends. The centurion of Matthew 8:5-13 understood this principle well, for he based his amazing statement of faith on the recognition that the Lord Jesus Christ represented the authority of the heavenly Father. With all the power of heaven behind Him, would not

---

*Bethany Fellowship, Minneapolis, 1970.

Jesus' word carry with it instant obedience in the unseen world? The centurion knew that his own word carried the authority of the Roman Empire behind it; he also realized that the power behind Jesus was far greater.

Scripture is rich with examples of those who were blessed by God for obedience to human authority, even when it would have been more convenient to disobey. David refused to kill King Saul on two occasions ominous with possibilities, on the grounds that Saul was the Lord's anointed. Saul was not even a good king, and David already knew he was God's choice to succeed Saul. However, David preferred to resist the temptation to do away with his mortal enemy, Saul, and continued to honor Saul's authority until the latter's death.

The Lord Jesus Himself, who had no earthly father, chose to submit to Joseph in the plan of God when he was found in the temple at the age of twelve while seeking to do the will of His heavenly Father. Samuel was a type of Christ in his submission to Eli, and it is said of both Jesus and Samuel that they increased in favor with God and men.

A life in divine order knows Jesus Christ as Lord, absolute "boss" over all human decisions. It accepts His estimate of family relationships and takes its place without question under the proper authority in its home. It reveres His Word and makes it not only the guideline for faith and conduct, but the final appeal in every argument. Such a life has the faith to say to those who question "why?"—"Because God says so." It knows no vacillating from the sure course of God's written Word off into the shoals of human tradition and opinion.

The Lord Jesus Christ is the supreme example of a life lived in such a way, for He never deviated at all from the pattern laid down for Him by His Father. Jesus never acted independently. He could say, "I have come down from heaven not to do My own will, but the will of Him who sent Me" (John 6:38). And in the great test in Gethsemane, seeking to find if there were any way He could avoid Calvary, He said, "Yet not My will, but Thine be done" (Luke 22:42).

One of the first lessons the Lord wants His people to learn is that we are not to act independently. His will for our lives involves our submission to His authority (i.e., quite literally confessing Him as Lord), and then being His person in all of our circumstances, submitting to the chain of command under which He has placed us. When we do this, we discover a strange and wonderful thing: we ourselves are then in a position to command respect from those answerable to us in the same chain. The essence of success in exercising authority, then, is to submit to authority ourselves.

Perhaps the biggest single problem in our culture today is that of floundering families. *U.S. News & World Report* (April 24, 1972) said there are 10,000 run-away children in the United States each week and that the divorce rate has climbed from one out of every four marriages to one out of three in the past decade. A current best seller in England makes in its title a poignant suggestion as to what is wrong: *The Death of the Family*.

Any thoughtful observer knows the home is in serious trouble, but few are willing to face the cause. Yet the increasing anarchy of our age did not develop in a vacuum. Within the past century, the Word of God has been attacked with a diabolical viciousness never before equaled. Liberal theology and permissiveness in education have given many the notion that biblical authority patterns are irrelevant and archaic in our time. In the massive, subtle attack upon our institutions, none has suffered so much as the family.

The man, once the unquestioned head of the home, is now relegated to a position of competition and even derision by his often more aggressive, dominating wife or mother. The woman, on the other hand, secretly longing for a man who will take his rightful role of leadership, feels that she is forced into decision-making and more forceful behavior simply because her husband has abdicated his role. More and more she finds him unbearably wishy-washy and ineffectual; he finds she is always running things, and more in despair and resignation than anything else, he lets her do it.

Stumbling through the maze of conflicts their parents pass on to them, the children become victims of the confusion. What they see may convince them that marriage is nothing but a guarantee of misery, and they will have none of it. They often buy the cheap philosophy of the "love-in," rationalizing that here, at least, they can walk out of it whenever it becomes hard.

God is looking for Christian couples who have the courage to swim upstream against the current of this destructive pattern which threatens to destroy society itself. Even in homes where only one mate knows Jesus Christ, the case is not hopeless. Not a few unsaved partners have been converted through the return of their believing husband or wife to a Biblical pattern of divine order. Where the unbelieving partner does not readily respond to the claims of Christ, the home situation can still be greatly improved by such positive action on the part of the one who is a child of God.

Very simply, God is looking for wives who will submit to their husbands and respect their husbands' authority (whether they deserve it or not), and for husbands who will love their wives with great unselfishness, as Christ loves the Church. Just as important, God wants each of us to fulfill our role as a member of the sex in which He created us. He wants masculine men and feminine women, and nothing short of this goal will satisfy Him.

The road back from the "unisex" swamp is the same approach which spells victory in any area of human life: to find out what God says and act on it. As we teach the children in Sunday School and Bible clubs, "God has said it, I believe it, and that's the end of it." Dogmatic? Yes, quite frankly so. It is the ancient issue of right and wrong, debated over and scoffed at so freely today. Yet all around us the bitter fruit of "situation ethics" and moral relativism gives mute testimony to the fact that God's word is right, and man is terribly wrong in trying to improve on it.

Our own family was no different from millions today. My husband and I suffered under a major confusion of our roles, even for the first decade after we were born again. Often I wondered whether keeping our home together was worth all the anguish and unfulfillment it cost both of us; certainly our children knew something was wrong, and they, too, were unhappy.

About two years ago we began to hear much teaching on divine order in the home. We decided the light we were getting was from God and we had better walk in it. One day the Holy Spirit spoke directly to my heart and told me to take a permanent back seat in the home. I had often been the decision maker; now I had to train myself to bite my lip, say nothing, and wait for my husband to step forward into his rightful place as leader.

It was not easy. At first Dick did not enjoy being forced into this position. We faced some unpleasant times and long silences while the children looked back and forth at both of us in obvious amusement.

The first specific area over which I abdicated an area of authority was the family budget. I turned over check books, bills and worries to my husband and have not troubled myself since with anything except the household money he gives me to spend.

One awkward incident occurred immediately after this transfer was made. The bank returned a rather large check which I had failed to record when I wrote it. The overdraft came in with the bank statement as a big surprise, and served to be God's way of proving to Dick that we had done the right thing. I really was as unfit for this job and as disinterested in it as I had been protesting for years!

Discipline of the children was the next big hurdle we faced. Christenson's book stresses that the father should administer punishment when he is in the home; the mother only in his absence. I had wanted this for years, and with such Biblical ammunition behind me, made my pronouncement: if Dick waited for me to punish the children in his presence, he'd be waiting until the Rapture!

The sea was really turbulent during the first few months of this new policy, but a new Daddy, increasingly less able to be manipulated by the children, began to emerge. I felt the real victory arrived the day he spanked one of the children for a poor attitude. It proved to be the most therapeutic punishment that the one had received in months, and was followed by a marked improvement in behavior.

Dick and I worked out an effective chore schedule for the children together, but he issued the edict that put the schedule into effect, and it has been he who has enforced it since. Now I do not have to be in the kitchen at dinner time except to cook and eat. One of the four sets the table, another clears, another loads the dishwasher, and the fourth scours the pots and cleans up the kitchen. We assign chores for six-month periods. In this way it is always easy to get after anyone who has forgotten to do his share. (No one has the excuse of not remembering it was his night to do a certain task!)

In the process of bringing our own home into divine order, I have discovered that it is now much easier to give my husband the respect Ephesians 5:33 commands, and Dick is certainly more devoted to me than ever. Both of us feel better about the example we are setting for our children, and especially for their opportunities to make good marriages themselves. I am much less subject to depression or negative moods than I used to be before I learned to submit to Dick.

Young people today need to realize that they are under authority which has been placed there by God Himself. To be subject to parents, teachers, employers and government is not a sign of weakness but rather of great strength. The Lord will bring great favor on any young person's life who dares to stand against the tide of rebellion in our culture today. One of the blessings such a young person will know is the joy of being master of his own passions, for the fruit of the Spirit includes self-control.

My brother Bill, now a missionary, served three years as a naval officer on an aircraft carrier. He led Bible studies for both officers and enlisted men, but found both groups greatly enlarged on the return half of the Far East cruise. The reason? So many men had observed the purity of his life and his refusal to indulge in immoral relationships while in port that they came to Bible study to find out his secret!

When people want to get free from demonic oppression, one of the first things we discuss with them is getting their authority patterns into divine order. We emphasize to them that it is only those who honor God's natural chain of command who can effectively submit to Him and resist the devil (James 4:7). If they resist this truth, we believe it will be hard for them to stay free after their initial deliverance, and we prefer not to minister to them.

However, where individuals are willing to do the will of God, truly wonderful things can happen to their lives and those of the members of their families. Only those who submit to rule are fit to rule. Every child of God will one day be in a position of authority over others in eternity (I Cor. 6:2, 3; Luke 19:11-27). The Lord intends that this life be our effective training ground for the life to come in His glorious kingdom.

4 Binding the Spirits

In addition to the obligation to bring our human relationships thoroughly into divine order, we have a sacred trust given us by the Lord to exercise the authority He gave us in the spiritual realm. The Bible teaches that a full, factual and final victory over Satan was won by the Lord Jesus Christ through His atoning death and resurrection. Even before Calvary, so irrevocable was the word of the "Lamb slain from the foundation of the world" (Rev. 13:8), that He could claim His victory as an established fact, and delegate His authority over the powers of darkness to his disciples. When His amazed followers came back with reports that the demons were subject to them in His name, the Lord told them that He had seen Satan fall from heaven. Then He gave them this extraordinary promise, this biggest of blank checks ever passed on to mere man, "Behold, I have given you authority to tread upon serpents and scorpions, and over all the power of the enemy, and nothing shall injure you" (Luke 10:19).

Very few Christians know what this means, for ever since Calvary the powers of darkness have made it their prime purpose to keep us from finding out. It is the old story of living destitute because we do not realize the spiritual fortune we have inherited in Christ. How sad is the plight of the believer who lives his entire Christian life in defeat because he believes the lies the enemy has told him.

The very first step out of this prison is to believe what God says. The key of His promise still unlocks the gate of Doubting Castle and releases us from the grip of Giant Despair. It is not enough to believe *in* God. We must *believe God*, or else we make Him a liar and fall into the tragic error of Eve—talking of God's Word, but acting on Satan's implanted doubts. Since God's word says that Jesus was truly manifested to destroy the works of the devil, that He led captivity captive, and that He gives us authority to tread on the powers of darkness, then we had better begin stomping! When we do, we will make this amazing discovery: It works!

An argument one frequently encounters when the believer's authority is taught is that the epistles do not teach it, only the gospels and Acts. Yet, the first chapter of Ephesians gives us a majestic, panoramic view of our full inheritance in Christ, and ends with the prayer that we shall come to know it in our earthly experience. There are five different Greek words connoting "power" in verse 19, and the sense of the passage which follows is that the Lord has delegated the authority to use this power to His body, the Church. In fact, the whole passage is a magnificent picture of divine order and authority: Christ seated at the right hand of God and thereby able to exercise His authority, then ourselves in Him, the body carrying out the will of the Head, and finally, under our feet (for the feet are part of the body) "all principality and power." These are the powers of darkness with which Paul says we wrestle (Ephesians 6:12). What a different attitude we shall have toward the battle once we realize that we face only defeated foes!

These are days in which the Lord is opening up the whole matter of body ministry. Perhaps a simple example will help to show what we mean. Suppose someone decides to take a walk. Can his brain or head do this for him? No, the feet must do the walking, but they will be unable to move until they get orders from the brain. Scientists tell us that every function of our body is inoperative without control and direction from some part of the brain. Perhaps it is for this reason that Scripture calls Christ "the Head" and the church "His body." We cannot function without vital union with Him, nor can we expect the Head to do the work of the hands and feet. It is in this latter area of our responsibility to act as the body of Christ that we have been so blinded by Satan and have so largely failed. Jesus notes this point with a different illustration in John 15:5: "I am the vine, you are the branches; he who abides in Me, and I in him, he bears much fruit; for apart from Me you can do nothing."

The first step toward fulfilling our proper function is to believe God. If He says that I am in Jesus as a member of His body, that the powers of darkness are beneath my feet, and that He has given me authority to tread on them then I can crush their activity at every turn, in Jesus' Name. I may be the most insignificant or newest believer—indeed, only a cell in a small toe of the body of Christ—but since evil powers are beneath my feet, too, I will do.

Now, instead of looking at circumstances from a purely human point of view, as any worldling can, one begins to deal with the unseen powers behind the circumstances. Is this not a basic purpose of prayer? We know that "the effective prayer of a righteous man can accomplish much" (James 5:16).

The Lord Jesus Christ has told us how to deal with demonic hindrances in Matthew 12:29. "Or how can anyone enter the strong man's house and carry off his property unless he first binds the strongman?"

Jesus often spoke of loosing people, for they had been bound by the enemy. However, He made it clear that we too have every right to bind the strong powers which have previously done the invisible chaining. These two passages together indicate that the most successful ministry of this kind is possible when two believers agree together on it. Together they join in heart and spirit with their risen Lord and bind the evil powers behind a given situation, at the same time loosing the people to do the will of God.

While I was typing these paragraphs my phone rang, and a sister in Christ who knows her authority in Him told me of a distressing problem in her church. It seems that the women's group has been plagued for two months by a member who causes strife and bitterness in each of the meetings. Together my friend and I agreed that this was the work of the enemy, bound him and his demons for a Monday night meeting coming up, and loosed the people to do the will of God, in order that they might reconcile and forgive one another. The victory was won; concord prevailed in the meeting.

Before entering a situation in which there is likely to be satanic or evil hindrance, we are to come against those powers responsible for such opposition in the name of Jesus. This involves more than just praying about the matter. We have to say to this mountain, "Be taken up and cast into the sea" (Mark 11:23). A direct approach is absolutely necessary. A suggested command is as follows: "By the authority of my risen Savior and Lord, I bind you, Satan, and all your evil powers disturbing this situation today, in the name of Jesus Christ. I command you to cease your maneuvers to hinder the Lord's will from being done." Results will be instantaneous and often dramatic.

A friend was asked to help out in a Vacation Bible School where discipline problems had become rampant. Most of the children were from under-privileged city homes and had not been previously exposed to the gospel. When this believer who knew her authority in Christ entered the building, the din and confusion were so great that she was able to speak out loud, binding the spirits as she walked down the aisle to the speaker's platform, without a soul realizing what she was doing. A hush immediately fell on the children, who listened attentively as she told the Bible story.

It is not necessary to bind the evil spirits in the presence of those in the situation you are considering; indeed, it is often not even wise. In the first place, demons communicate by telepathy or ESP. In the second place, it is a rare group that you will find prepared to hear such commands addressed directly to the powers of darkness. The enemy would like nothing better than to stir up controversy because of misunderstanding resulting from such a move. We are to be wise as serpents and harmless as doves. In no area is this caution more important than when dealing with the powers of darkness.

During a regular Thursday morning Bible study in 1970, my telephone rang. It was Jerry Myers, husband of one of the women present, calling to tell Lois of a desperate situation he had just observed nearby. A man clad in a black cloak was striding up and down a narrow ledge high up on the State Office Building in Albany, getting ready to jump. Jerry had bound the demons in the situation, and then felt prompted to call us so that our whole group could join in agreement. This we did, addressing the spirit of *suicide* specifically and commanding its activity nullified in the name of the Lord Jesus Christ.

That night the news media recorded the fact that, shortly before noon, the man stopped striding back and forth and meekly climbed back in the window of the building—just minutes after the spirits were bound. The reports also included this interesting fact: never before, in the long history of suicides from its ledge, had this building ever received back a potential victim!

Such poignant examples can be found by anyone who will act on these principles. We are to be "doers of the Word, and not merely hearers who delude themselves" (James 1:22).

It would be misleading to give the impression that binding the spirits is to be reserved only for small, individual situations. Many of us believe that we are now moving into an era in God's plan when we will bind the demon princes who hold entire cities, and all their underlings. We will then have the great corollary privilege of loosing people within those cities who are hungry for God.

"Truly I say to you, whatever you shall bind on earth shall have been bound in heaven; and whatever you loose on earth shall have been loosed in heaven. Again I say to you, that if two of you agree on earth about anything that they may ask, it shall be done for them by My Father who is in heaven. For where two or three have gathered together in My name, there I am in their midst." (Matthew 18:18-20)

Such moves are not to be entered into lightly, though. They are only for obedient saints who walk in humility with their glorified, risen Lord, and have sought Him thoroughly for His answer and His timing in a given situation. Fasting is not only appropriate in such times, but perhaps even necessary (Isaiah 58:6). If we are unwilling to deny the routine appetites of the flesh for at least brief periods of time, we have certainly not yet realized that we are to be soldiers in a great warfare. Hedonism has no place in those who would bind vast armies in the unseen world. The apostle Paul understood this well when he wrote, "Suffer hardship with me, as a good soldier of Christ Jesus. No soldier in active service entangles himself in the affairs of everyday life, so that he may please the one who enlisted him as a soldier" (II Tim. 2:3, 4).

Perhaps the most dramatic application of this principle in my own experience was in connection with the massive demonstration of young radicals in Washington, D.C., during the

May Day weekend in 1971. I was attending a charismatic conference in Fairfax, Virginia, the week prior to the May Day activities. There I met a perceptive believer who had had a vision of the Capitol building a few nights before. She had seen it loom before her with a huge American Indian spirit poised over its dome. She felt prompted to share this revelation with a group so that we might agree together to bind that spirit in the name of Jesus Christ, which we did.

It is now history that the widespread destruction planned for that weekend never amounted to much. Yet police and other government agencies were expecting serious trouble, and were relieved that the weekend did not include great bloodshed.

The most diabolical of human plans require demonic aid for their completion; hence the relative impotence of the human vessels when they are not so aided. A good example of binding the spirits in a situation which seemed hopeless for many years was in the recent end of United States involvement in the Vietnam war and release of our prisoners of war. Countless Christians had been praying to these ends for years. However, some months before the cease fire, our New Testament Fellowship began binding the spirits in this situation, and we are confident that God led other groups to do the same thing.

Perhaps the release of millions of prisoners behind the Iron and Bamboo curtains can be brought about in a similar way. Certainly such a desperate need makes it worthwhile for believers everywhere to seek God about His will and timing in such exercise of our authority. We can trust God to instruct us when, where and how to act in binding the powers of darkness and loosing human wills from their grip.

In recent weeks we have received mailings from two excellent organizations seeking to provide help of various kinds for persecuted Christians in communist countries: Open Doors with Brother Andrew (P.O. Box 2020, Orange, California, 92669) and Jesus to the Communist World. (P.O. Box 11, Glendale, California, 91209). There is no doubt in my mind that prayer support for such endeavors is near to the heart of God. However, such moves without correlative moves binding the spirits behind the oppression of Christians could prove heartbreaking. We, as the Church of Jesus Christ, need to bind the spirits directly oppressing persecuted believers as well as those operating through their human oppressors. At the same time we can open for the believers the greatest possible spiritual freedom in the midst of their circumstances, and pray that their oppressors do the will of God in each case.

The Lord will probably allow still more to receive the supreme crown of martyrdom, as did twenty-year-old Vanya described in the February-March, 1973, *Open Doors*. However, perhaps there will be fewer of the other type of tragic case described in the magazine: a believer imprisoned for years for her faith who succumbed to the terrible pressures of the concentration camp and denied her Lord.

It is well to remember that everywhere in the New Testament we are exhorted to pray for believers and to do all that we can for the household of faith. Even the exhortation to pray for earthly rulers and authorities is "in order that we may lead a tranquil and quiet life in all godliness and dignity" (I Timothy 2:2). When Paul wrote these words, he was a prisoner of the Roman Empire, awaiting his own execution for the sake of Jesus Christ.

God is giving us hints in these days that He plans to surprise some of the citadels of atheism with His hand of judgment. No communist edict could produce the grain that God withheld from both China and Russia this past year (1972). Suppose this lack, which reduced those nations to unprecedented trade with the free world to get life-saving grain, proves but the harbinger of much more serious famine ahead? The United States, Canada, and Australia may then well find ourselves in the position of Joseph in the time of the famine of Egypt—and able to demand our own terms for the release of such grain!

If Christians intercede as never before, bind the spirits as God directs us, and communicate to government leaders and lawmakers our will concerning our desire for freedom of religious prisoners in those parts of the world needing food, who can tell what God may do? Part of our problem in seeing so little done in the world for the cause of righteousness is believing God for so little. Today the Lord is looking for those who will scoff at impossibilities and keep a firm eye of faith upon God and His Word. Only as He has those who meet His conditions can He gloriously prove how literally true are such promises as these:

"Truly I say to you, whoever *says* to this mountain, 'Be taken up and cast into the sea,' and does not doubt in his heart, but believes that what he says is going to happen; it shall be granted him. Therefore I say to you, all things for which you pray and ask, believe that you have received them, and they shall be granted you." (Mark 11:23, 24)

Sections for chapters 3 and 4 have been reprinted by permission from the author's article, "Is There A Filiarchy Near You?" in the Jan.-Feb., 1972, issue of *The Christian Teacher,* Box 550, Wheaton, Illinois (60187).

5 | Discerning of Spirits

A problem which has bothered many is how believers who are using spiritual gifts can at times do such foolish things. One would expect those who are baptized in the Holy Spirit and conscious of His presence and leading in their lives to make very few mistakes. Yet the reverse sometimes is true. Moreover, it is not uncommon for such believers to preface a wrong move with such a statement as "The Lord led me to do this," or, "God told me to tell you this."

Such a remark puts an awkward burden on the hearer. If he rejects the idea, he implies that he is rejecting God's will. If he accepts it, he may be receiving wrong guidance as well as encouraging another believer in an erroneous practice. For the one who claims infallible guidance the danger is even worse. Pride may sweep in, establishing a powerful beachhead in his life. If that believer then becomes unteachable, much of his usefulness to the Lord is lost.

How can we avoid such a dilemma? One very obvious way is to refrain from telling anyone that "the Lord is leading us" to pursue a given action. In this way we are freed from the temptation to blame God for our own foolishness, but we are still able to give God the glory if our guidance proves genuine.

When we act unwisely, it is important to realize that we are responsible. We confess our sin to God in order to enjoy His bountiful love and forgiveness in unbroken fellowship. Notions of infallibility put us on dangerous ground.

Our verbal testimony about divine guidance is only the tip of an iceberg, however. The bulk of the problem lies in the unwelcome fact that we can be wrongly led spiritually. The Word of God warns of this danger in many passages and gives us clear ways to protect ourselves. Because some Christians refuse to heed these warnings, many projects begun in the will of God have bogged down in the quagmire of satanic deception.

It is well to know that Satan and his minions are battling for the mind of the believer. This is why Scripture stresses, "Watch over your heart with all diligence, for from it flow the springs of life" (Proverbs 4:23); "as he thinks within himself, so he is" (Proverbs 23:7). Often our conversation reveals just what kind of thoughts we have, no matter how cleverly we feel we can conceal them. "For the mouth speaks out of that which fills the heart" (Matt. 12:34).

Years ago in Africa I was puzzled by a fellow missionary who seemed to resent spiritual discussions of any kind. She was uneasy and hostile until a conversation would turn to secular matters. Once she confided to me that the only way she could stand life on the field was to take tranquilizers three times a day. When this unfortunate friend left Africa, she ordered her possessions to be sold. To their amazement, her fellow workers found many boxes full of cheap love stories and detective thrillers among her things. These were the thoughts that filled her mind and rendered it daily less fit for God's service.

Today the phenomenon of defeated Christians is with us on every hand, many of whom will not even take the trouble to read. An inquiry about such a person's daily habits often reveals long, vacant hours spent in front of the television set, imbiding some of the worst ideas the world has to offer. Women sometimes spend vain hours on the telephone, gossiping and indulging in self-pity. Men find themselves being sucked into wrong companionships at work in plant or office, often listening to off-color jokes and cynical conversations. Both sexes could turn these areas of defeat into opportunities for witness, if their minds were saturated with the Word of God. Yet such people seldom see their lives in the light of Psalm 1:1-3, God's revealed secret of the life of victory.

"How blessed is the man who does not walk in
 the counsel of the wicked,
Nor stand in the path of sinners,
Nor sit in the seat of scoffers!
But his delight is in the law of the Lord,
And in His law he meditates day and night.
And he will be like a tree firmly planted by
 streams of water,
Which yields its fruit in its season,
And its leaf does not wither;
And in whatever he does, he prospers."

Very simply summarized, this passage declares that a happy, godly man is one who does not follow the advice of the unconverted, nor find himself in agreement and close fellowship with the enemies of God. He is one who delights in Scripture, dwelling in it day and night. His life shows

God's favor by the way that he is successful in doing what he attempts for God.

Now by these standards many Christians will fail to pass the test. The non-spiritual ones will fail in verse one; the super-spiritual ones who have followed false leadings will be shown up easily by verses two and three. The latter, however tragically earnest they may be, are often experience-centered and will not obey the revealed Word of God; furthermore, they sometimes care very little to change the situation by getting into the hard work of Bible study and application to the life.

The late Ulric Jelinek, scientist and lay preacher, used to say that anyone who means business with God should read His Word once through every year. Such a schedule entails three chapters each weekday, and five each Sunday. (Years ago I discovered a system which works beautifully for the purpose; it follows in chapter 8.) Those who decide to discipline themselves into God's pattern will soon discover what these words of the Lord Jesus mean: "If you abide in My word, then you are truly disciples of Mine; and you shall know the truth, and the truth shall make you free" (John 8:31, 32).

The transformation and renewing of our minds which we are called to in Romans 12:1 and 2 requires a displacement of our own negative thinking with God's thoughts—His Word. Anyone who is truly serious about wanting liberty in the spirit and ability to discern between good and evil spirits must dwell in the Word of God. In this way we become accustomed to God's ways and principles, as well as His specific deeds and laws. In time we have a sense of rightness or wrongness about given situations or people, not based on anything as flimsy as human intuition, but on the revealed Word of God.

For those who want to have Jesus as *Lord* of their lives and live by His Word, there is a particular ministry and gift of the Holy Spirit which is designed to determine spiritual origin. The gift of discerning or distinguishing of spirits is mentioned as one of the nine gifts of the Holy Spirit in I Corinthians 12: 9 and 10. This gift is coming into increasing prominence and usage in the contemporary charismatic movement because of the great need on every hand. How does it work? What may we expect if we ask God to give us this gift?

Well, first of all it is important to realize that the gift is in the Holy Spirit—not a separate package neatly wrapped up for us to take and use, disregarding all the other eight gifts. It is essential that we ask God to fill us with His Holy Spirit; then we may be sure that He will distribute to us such usage of the gifts as He wills (I Corinthians 12:11). Perhaps we should add here that we cannot dictate to God. It is folly indeed to pray or secretly think, "Lord, I want the gift of discerning of spirits, but I don't want the tongues." Such a statement may reveal what Scripture calls "an evil heart of unbelief" (Hebrews 3:12), and could put a barrier between ourselves and a Holy God who warns us that iniquity can prevent our prayers from being heard and answered (Isaiah 59:2).

Secondly, God gives to us, as someone has said, "according to our need, not our greed." We shall find we have this gift operative in our lives when we need it in ministry or occasions demanding discerning of spirits. We do not just walk around with this gift as a possession, able to use it by an act of our own will. Rather, the potential is there for us to draw upon, from the infinite resources of the Holy Spirit, when He ascertains that there is a need for its use. Sometimes He will make us aware of His checks and warnings in this area even when we are unaware of a need for this kind of help.

Let me give an example of what I mean. Recently in our New Testament Fellowship a visitor started coming who had a background of teaching and preaching. It so happened that we had a need for speakers around that time, and our board was seriously considering using this man. Yet three of us, absolutely independent of one another, discerned a spirit of heresy in him. To appreciate this fully, we must clarify that nothing he said or did in our group indicated his error. The warning was entirely supernatural and was given to those of us who are frequently used of God to manifest the gift of discerning of spirits. Each of us told members of the church board of our concern, and on that basis the man was not approached to teach.

Some weeks later we found that the visitor was involved with the "Jesus Only" heresy. How grateful we were to God for His mercy and supernatural revelation which spared us the cancer of that error being spread in our group. How much we need the gift of discerning of spirits when we assemble together as Christians, since "the Spirit explicitly says that in later times some will fall away from the faith, paying attention to deceitful spirits and doctrines of demons." (I Timothy 4:1)

Not all evil spirits are concerned with wrong doctrine, however. In another incident, a charismatic group was troubled by a sense of coldness and lack of spiritual power for some months. Finally the group sought God for the reason, and one man blurted out that he had "violent disagreement" with certain members of the group over methods of ministry. He shared his views with those with whom he disagreed and with the elders of the group. Yet he could not seem to overcome his problem with resentment. Again the group sought the Lord and asked Him for guidance. Several members of the group had the term, "a spirit of jealousy," come to their minds. As they shared these experiences, it was generally felt that this was the man's problem. However, to make certain that they were not wrongly using or interpreting this gift, they asked God to take care of the problem in His way. Soon the man disassociated himself from the group, and the former warmth and spiritual life of the body of believers returned.

This example will show several things about the gift of discerning of spirits. First, it is often given to solve a problem in a group of Christians by pointing to the unseen enemy behind that problem. Secondly, it is seldom if ever a private revelation. God sees to it that several in a given group receive the same information, which serves to confirm it to the whole group. Thirdly, it is not a gift which can be used without the operation of other gifts as well. When the presence of an evil spirit has been verified by the Holy Spirit and its identity named, there is still need for the word of wisdom to know what to do about such knowledge. The ideal situation (and the one, happily, that we usually see) is that the person is able to face up to the presence of that spirit so that he may renounce it and cast it out or have it cast out. (See chapter 6 for details on this subject.) However, when the person is unwilling to face up to his problem, as was the case in each of the two examples just given, the church or body of believers locally must decide what to do about the situation to avoid harm to the whole group. In both of these incidents just described, God's word of wisdom came to wait; very soon He removed both men from these respective groups. Sometimes, however, God will require the elders to take disciplinary action.

One such case with which I am familiar took place some years ago in a church which was not charismatic. A certain individual disrupted the prayer meetings by praying for twenty minutes or more each time, often in a preachy and condemnatory manner for the sake of exhorting others who were present. Finally many people stopped coming to the prayer meeting, and it became evident to the church board that this woman was being used by the enemy to hinder God's work. She had to be approached by the ruling body of men and asked to leave the church. It seems clear that this woman was obsessed by some religious demons, for she was so deluded that she thought the elders called her in for the purpose of calling her to preach. Had the supernatural gift been in operation in the congregation, it is probable that her problem would have been discerned far earlier and dealt with before it became such a serious matter.

Up to this point we have examined how God protects the body of believers by giving them usage of the gift of discerning of spirits for others. However, by far the most serious need of the charismatic Christian today is to know how to discern or recognize an evil spirit influencing himself. To locate and identify such enemies within the body of Christ is the most important exercise of this same gift. Whether individual groups and assemblies recognize this fact and learn to discern spirits in their midst could well be the determining factor of their success or failure in these last days before the return of the Lord Jesus Christ.

In medical practice it is considered folly for a doctor to allow a diagnosed cancer to remain and grow unhindered. In like manner it is surely folly for members of Christ's body to allow evil spirits to remain in them once they have been found. How do we know when we are vexed, harrassed, oppressed, or even obsessed by demons? How can we be sure that the gift of discerning of spirits is used accurately in our own local body of believers?

The Word of God lists the gift of discerning of spirits in a context which includes eight other gifts intended for body ministry. Thus, we can find no excuse for the common flip dismissal of this gift as needed only to minister to unbelievers. If this gift were to be exercised so differently from all the others, surely the Holy Spirit would have included such instruction in First Corinthians 12-14. We conclude that this gift was to be used, as were all the others, in ministering to both believers and unbelievers in the group. Experience has taught us that this gift, like all the others, is primarily used for believers in providing knowledge necessary for setting them free.

We are daily coming to appreciate the mighty gift of discerning of spirits more and more. Although it is not necessary for locating a compulsive attitude or habit of which one is aware in his life, it is invaluable in identifying demonic torment of which we are unaware.

Let me give an example. For four long years after my own initial deliverance from an evil spirit, I knew I was still seriously bound. Yet pray and agonize as I did, I could not locate the source of the difficulty. Then in March, 1970, we learned much more about deliverance in this area through the one-night ministry of Don Basham. Soon afterward we began having group deliverance services for people needing help, and after the very first of these I went to bed very tense. As I asked God what the problem was, I closed my eyes. To my amazement, with my mind's eye I suddenly saw SELF-PITY spelled before me in great capital letters. I renounced this spirit and commanded it to leave me, and not only was relaxed in body but underwent the greatest change in my personality I had ever known apart from my conversion experience.

It is my firm conviction that this spirit was the key or ruler spirit in my life, and evidently it was so much a part of me that I never would have guessed it to be an intruder apart from the supernatural revelation of the Holy Spirit. In other words, had I been aware of feeling sorry for myself much of the time (which I was not), I would have assumed it to be a problem in the flesh.

We are told plainly in Hebrews 4:12 that only the living Word can divide soul and spirit; thus His gift is doubtless intended to reveal which problems we have are demonic (and therefore require the word of command to depart) and which are simply problems in the flesh or carnal nature (requiring putting them off and reckoning ourselves dead to them).

Countless times since my own deliverance from the spirit of *self-pity*, we have been privileged to see the Lord move in a similar sovereign way to deliver others. Once a brilliant intellectual who was quite psychotic was brought to us for help. He could easily out-talk and out-reason any of our body of believers. Yet he was invisibly chained by the merciless bonds of a spirit of *pride* whose identity was revealed to three of our group at once, and on this basis he renounced it, we cast it out, and the Lord set him free.

Once a man came for help who had tried to live an exemplary Christian life. Yet he was caught in the bonds of a vicious lust that would give him no peace day or night. He was too ashamed to mention the nature of his torment, but was delivered of it later while intercession was offered for him in the prayer language. Here, evidently the Holy Spirit not only identified the demon but also commanded it to go as the unsuspecting intercessor did all that he knew how to do. In this case a *spirit of lust* was involved, not just a fleshly desire, for the man felt a slithering presence leave his body.

Sometimes we are not given a word to identify a spirit which is troubling someone, but rather a mental picture or an idea. Often a demon is discerned by observers as it confesses itself through the tormented person. Once a woman said, "Oh, I wouldn't feel so guilty if I didn't hate my mother. I've always hated my mother. I can't remember when I didn't hate my mother." The spirit confessing itself here was the spirit of *hate*, but before this woman could be delivered from it she had to forgive her mother. This example shows how the Holy Spirit will reveal several different things at once during a time of ministry: the identity of the spirit, and the ground or reason in the believer's life that this torment has been permitted to stay. All that the Holy Spirit reveals has to be applied and obeyed if a person hopes to stay free.

It is my firm conviction that God is revealing the identity of evil spirits to countless believers everywhere in these days, and they are not aware of it. When words which describe negative attitudes or torments cross our minds, we are often being given discerning of spirits so that we will do something about them! If it is for ourselves or someone who is open to deliverance, we should share this information with the person and help him to get free. If the person appears to be closed to that kind of help, we can then bind that spirit and keep it from ruining a given situation.

When a tormented person is spreading false guidance or false prophecy because of leadings from an evil source, it seems imperative that the individual be approached and warned, as well as those that person is trying to influence. A few questions might serve to clarify such situations: Is the guidance *compulsive;* in other words, did the person have to do it with no power to control himself? Does the message of prophecy or interpretation of tongues draw attention to the giver of the message or to the Lord Jesus Christ?

Is the message condemnatory? Is there a falsetto quality to the voice of the message-giver, or contortions in facial expression? Is information given which amounts to individual fortune-telling, rather than comfort or edification for the believers (I Cor. 14:3)?

If the answer to any of the above questions is yes, it would be very wise for the body to consider that fact a warning: a time to stop, look, and listen to the guidance of the Lord as to how to handle the situation. No better time could be found for asking God for an exercise of discerning of spirits, a word of wisdom, knowledge, faith, or any other gift which may prevent havoc or chaos in the body of Christ.

If the person giving a prophecy refuses to allow it to be judged (I Cor. 14:29), or if someone is approached about leading others astray with false guidance who fails to heed, there can be no continuing fellowship with that individual.

"Reject a factious man after a first and second warning, knowing that such a man is perverted and is sinning, being self-condemned." (Titus 3:10, 11)

6 Casting Out Spirits

When the Lord Jesus Christ began His earthly ministry and called His disciples, He commanded them to continue in fellowship with Him, to preach, and to cast out demons (Mark 3:14, 15). Had these simple instructions been obeyed over the ages, the church could have been saved much heartache. Praise God that we live in a day when this simple yet powerful way is again becoming the norm for thousands of believers.

Possibly the greatest heresy the devil has ever injected into the church is the notion that all demons leave a human personality once he has received Christ as His Savior and Lord. We must affirm again, as at the beginning of this book, that all we ever get from God is what we appropriate by faith. Clearly the Lord Jesus regarded casting out demons as a necessary ministry which should accompany the preaching of the gospel. Where this is being done, new believers are freed from their compulsive hangups and obsessive wrong thoughts as they *start* the Christian life, not after years of failure. But let me hasten to add, (as one believer who waited nearly a decade after conversion to have the first demon cast out of me) better late than never!

Proof of the statement that not all demons leave at conversion* can be found in the fact that most church and mission boards go to elaborate means to cover up cases of severe sexual aberration (sometimes among leaders) which they discover. Sometimes the tormented individuals have been so used of God that there is no question about their being born again. The only real question is why do they behave as they do? When a believer dwells in the Word of God and prays earnestly for victory over some sin in his life, it seems to us that there is no other answer to his dilemma apart from deliverance from evil spirits.

However, let us hasten to add, this explanation is not tantamount to giving a person license to continue with his behavior under some such lame excuse as, "the devil made me do it." Oh no! Once the demons, are cast out, the person then has the responsibility to walk with the Lord and keep them out, crucifying the sinful thought life of the old carnal nature that would invite them back. Deliverance from evil spirits can be a wide open door to the life of victory, but not a magic cure from temptation, which would conveniently bypass the need for self-discipline.

It is well to remember that demons are disembodied spirits which seek human bodies through which they can express their evil attitudes, appetites, and afflictions. Often they enter through occult experimentation, unforgiveness, or great emotional stress on the part of the person. Frequently they remain in a family line which they have previously succeeded in attacking through

*Don Basham, *Can A Christian Have A Demon* (Monroeville, Pa. Whitaker, 1971).

one of these means. Descendants of such ancestors sometimes find themselves tormented; they may be caught in a snare for which they are not responsible, and from which they fear they cannot escape. Praise Jesus! There is an escape. But, like all other things God does, it must be handled His way.

In the Old Testament era we find no recorded cure for demonic oppression. God required the death penalty for those who practiced the occult arts. (See Exodus 22:18 and Leviticus 20:27). Apparently the danger to Israel if they intermingled wih demon-controlled people was so great that God ordered Israel to exterminate the Canaanites to protect them (Deut. 18:9-14). The failure of he Hebrew nation to obey this command fully was responsible for their downfall, over and over again. Only in the very severe judgment of the Babylonian Captivity did Israel finally learn her lesson. That dose of punishment did cure her of idolatry.

With the coming of the Lord Jesus Christ, a new day dawned for the demon-harassed. Early in His earthly ministry Jesus began casting out demons, and He instructed His followers to do likewise, in His Name. Chapter 10 of Luke's gospel is a poignant account of the thrill and amazement Jesus' disciples felt when they found they could expel demons in His Name.

This ministry is a prominent characteristic of the New Testament era. We can be very thankful that we live on this side of Calvary, for the Lord Jesus has completed His work of human redemption by destroying the power of the devil (I John 3:8). However, it is well to remember that His work is finished. The Lord Jesus Christ does not need to do one more thing about the devil and his demon powers. He expects us to believe His Word when He tells us that He led captivity captive and gave gifts unto men (Eph. 4:8), and He also expects us to rout the demons in His Name just as He commanded (Mark 16:17).

A pastor once told me that he and his elders met daily for two years to pray for the deliverance of a tormented woman in his congregation; yet as far as he knew, that prayer was never answered. Of course not! For these men, however earnest, were disobedient to the revealed will of God. The ministry of deliverance from evil spirits is effected by casting out, although prayer and fasting are also sometimes necessary (Mark 9:29). We need not beg God to do what He has plainly told us to do. It is just as simple as that. Only unbelief hinders present-day disciples from exercising their authority over demons, just as unbelief was the prime hindrance among Jesus' own disciples when they encountered a difficult case (Matt. 17:20).

For some reason contemporary Christians find it quite difficult to accept the fact that born-again believers can be tormented by demons. Some have admitted that they have run into this problem on the mission field (see *Power for Living*, published by Scripture Press, January 16, 1972), but many are still tragically naive about the reality of demonic oppression among believers right here at home. The source of this "blind spot" is the prince of darkness himself, who fears nothing so much as the awakening of the Church to her total power and authority over him and his demons.

Two years ago a friend had been losing consciousness and having violent dizzy spells for several weeks. Although exhaustive medical tests revealed nothing, she was forbidden to drive. A demon of epilepsy was cast out of her during one of our first group deliverance meetings in this area, and she has been fine ever since.

Stella was another believer who had severe problems. Emotionally very tense, she found herself unable to control a hideous laughter during prayer meetings. The laugh never occurred again after a demon called *madness* was cast out. Stella has since been delivered of many evil spirits, and today is as calm and radiant as she was once tormented. Before her deliverance, Stella was a compulsive talker. Now she is a wonderful listener who counsels many troubled Christians with their problems, often teaching them how to cast out demons from their own lives.

Satan has provoked a very clever controversy over a commonly-used term which is based on an unfortunate rendering of the King James Bible translators. The Greek New Testament word *daimonizomai* simply means, quite literally, "be demonized." However, the King James and other English Bibles translate this verb "be demon possessed." In modern English the word "possession" carries with it the connotation of ownership, and this is the point of the controversy. Since the Lord Jesus Christ owns the Christian, having paid for him with His own blood, it is obviously impossible for Satan or any demon to own a believer. This exaggerated interpretation "possession", is prejudicial against one who "is demonized." In John 8:48 the Gospel writer speaks of "having" a demon, while in 10:21 he uses "demonized" in the very same sense as in the earlier verse. "Having" a demon and being "demon-possessed" clearly do not sound synonymous in English. And confusion of the two concepts is inappropriate, at the very least.

The difficulty comes in the assumed deduction that if a demon is within a person's body, the demon is in full control of that body. This is very seldom the case; in my opinion it is never the case for a born-again Christian in whom the Spirit of God dwells. It is a gross oversimplification to say that the Spirit of God and demon spirits cannot occupy the body of a believer at the same time. Notions of geography just do not apply to spiritual things. Who is to say what part of the believer the demon actually controls, and what part the Holy Spirit controls? The many admonitions in Scripture to crown Jesus completely Lord of our lives would seem to indicate that the issue is by no means settled at the time of conversion.

My husband and I own a deed to the home in which we live. This deed does not guarantee that a thief will be unable to sneak into our home at three o'clock in the morning and steal some of our goods. Invasion into our home by an intruder is always possible, even though it is quite undesirable. One thing is certain, though: if a thief does break in, we would hardly give the deed to him! Quite the contrary. Our sole interest would be to oust him as quickly as possible. So it is in the deliverance ministry.

When the Lord freed the crippled woman from her condition, He diagnosed her problem as having a spirit of infirmity (Luke 13:11-16). It is also significant that Jesus called her "a daughter of Abraham" though she had been "bound" by Satan for eighteen years. During a controversy with the Pharisees in the eighth chapter of John, the Lord denied their claim to the term, "sons of Abraham." He noted that they were the "seed" of Abraham, but not his "children," for they did not love the Son of God. In fact, He plainly stated that their father was the devil. This line of thought is prominent in the Pauline epistles. All who have Abraham's faith are said to have him as their father (Romans 4:16), and all who belong to Christ are Abraham's only true seed and heirs (Galatians 3:29).

Actually, most people attending deliverance meetings are Christians. Usually they are committed believers who have been puzzled for years about certain areas in their lives or thought patterns which are inconsistent with their testimony of new life in Christ. On one notable occasion an unbeliever was present during such a meeting. Nothing effective happened until she left. Even the Lord Jesus Himself did few mighty works in Nazareth "because of their unbelief" (Matt. 13:58).

I learned about the reality of demonic oppression the only way some of us ever learn anything—the hard way. In 1966 I was flown home from an African mission field three months early for furlough, a physical, emotional and spiritual wreck. There was a rare parasitic disease in my lymph glands, my body was emaciated, and I had lost my will to live.

A few weeks after I got home, I picked up an issue of *Christian Life* magazine describing the plight of believers caught in a web of demonic torment. The author declared that people could be released from their bondage when the demons vexing them were cast out in Jesus' Name. Great light turned on my darkened soul. I knew I needed deliverance from evil spirits.

God saw to it that I got the help I needed, but it came little by little over a period of years. First He led me to people who knew how to cast out spirits. They used a method of counseling to find out the identity of the demons. After talking with me for two days (during which time I fasted), they discovered that I was obsessed with ideas concerning future happenings. Then they cast out a *lying spirit of prophecy* and wisely advised me to pay no attention to impressions on my mind involving future events.

Before long I felt much better and gained back the thirty-five pounds I had lost. However, for several years I struggled with depression, tenseness, and a vicious temper. The great breakthrough in my life came in 1970, but the telling of that story is another whole book (*OUT! In the Name of Jesus*, published by Creation House, 1973). Suffice it to say here that God is teaching many of His children today the things that we learned at such great cost. The answer for many children of God is to have demons cast out of them which should have been banished long ago, had they only known what to do.

Contrary to popular belief, we have learned

that taking authority over evil spirits should be a first move toward solving a problem, not a last resort. Here again, God's Word is the standard. Jesus did not wait until He got an especially spiritual group off to a deeper life convention to unveil the mysteries about evil spirits and cast them out. Quite the contrary! Everywhere He went, He preached the gospel, healed the sick, and cast out demons. He did it as a matter of course immediately on entering an area. He never entertained any arguments about whether there were evil spirits or not; He simply cast them out.

Another thing that Jesus Christ did not do was take the people aside for very private, hush-hush counseling when He cast demons out of them. He seemed totally unconcerned about their embarrassment about the process of getting free; His entire emphasis was on their deliverance itself and resultant change in the life. Jesus cast out demons from the people in the groups where He found them and where they met Him; His disciples found out it worked the same way for them when they challenged the spirits in His Name (Luke 10).

Occasionally one has a request from a tormented person who would rather have a "private session" for deliverance; perhaps there is nothing wrong with this idea if no one else is around who understands and believes in the Lord's current ability to meet such needs through the ministry of His people. However, if the person intends to keep his deliverance quiet afterward, he has a very poor prognosis for staying free. It was not an insignificant matter that the Lord Jesus told the Gadarene demoniac to "Go home to your people and report to them what great things the Lord has done for you, and how He had mercy on you" (Mark 5:19).

Evil powers work in darkness; "God is light, and in Him there is no darkness at all" (I John 1:5). Just as turning over damp, mossy rocks and exposing them to the sunshine will send the swarming vermin beneath them scurrying for darkness, so our cheerful testimony of deliverance will send demons in dismay looking for someone who cannot be so honest. God's Word has this powerful victory formula for saints over the ages who will be found to have victory over Satan:

> "And they overcame him because of the blood of the Lamb and because of the word of their testimony, and they did not love their life even to death." (Revelation 12:11)

We cannot claim the protection of the blood of Jesus Christ and see it avail in our lives if we are unwilling to share the word of our testimony with others, caring nothing of what they think of us in the process. Our Lord made it powerfully simple when He said He will deny those before the Father who deny Him before men (Matthew 10:32, 33).

How do we know we need deliverance from evil spirits? How may we be sure of success in this area of ministry? What kind of preparation do we need before spirits are cast out? How we can we stay free once we have been exorcised?

Perhaps a simple acrostic will help us to remember some basic facts in answering these questions and helping others. A person who is bound wants to be set *free*; hence we have chosen that word to stress these four important points:

F—Forgive everyone, living or dead, whom we have ever resented (Matt. 18:21-35).

R—Renounce all occult practices, and burn or destroy all occult games, books, or objects (Deut. 18:10-14; Acts 19:18-20); renounce and confess any such sins of ancestors (Lev. 26:40-42).

E—Expel demons by name in direct verbal attack against them in the name of Jesus Christ (Mark 5: 8,9; Mark 9:25; Acts 16: 16-18).

E—Exert our human will in line with God's will from then on, by:
1) praising God (II Chron. 20: 21, 22; Psalm 149)
2) dwelling in His Word (John 8:31,32; Psalm 119) and obeying it, and
3) putting on the whole armor of God (Ephesians 6:10-18).

When Christians are exposed to teaching like that in this book and especially in this chapter, their reactions are a good indication as to whether they have need for deliverance or not. Feelings of anxiety, excessive drowsiness, nausea, tremors, headache, or other sudden physical symptoms are a fair indication that there is a need for having demons cast out. The reaction of fear which many will experience is not actually a human reaction at all, but that of the spirits who are afraid of expulsion from their home.

If the reader is experiencing such discomfort at the present time, cheer up! This is a good sign. Probably the heart is tender to the Lord and ready to be dealt with in a way that will make the pathway to full deliverance easier.

However, if the main reaction is one of skepticism, violent negativism, or hostility, *and there is* virtually *no sense of need in the life* we would suggest that you leave this whole subject alone for a while. Ask God to show you if you have need, and read through the New Testament again looking for teaching on this subject. If you are a child of God, He will surely show you what He wants for your life.

Now for those who feel they do have a need, and want to know how to go about having it met, we offer the following suggestions. Get a group of likeminded Christians together with you, all of whom have had some recent teaching on this subject. We suggest my own book, *OUT! In The Name of Jesus*, or Don Basham's book, *Deliver Us From Evil*, as excellent for this purpose. A tape or casette on deliverance heard immediately prior to ministry together is also an excellent faith builder.

Find a time when all of you can spend at least two hours together. Fast if at all possible beforehand (Isaiah 58:6-8). Open your time in praise and prayer, taking several minutes just to bless the Lord and affirm your faith in Him. A petition for His guidance might go something like this: "Father God, we ask your guidance and blessing upon this meeting as You set Your people free. We claim the protection of the blood of Jesus Christ upon every member of every family represented here, and upon all members of the family of God everywhere. We thank You that we come against only defeated foes; that the

Son of God was manifested for this purpose, to destroy the works of the devil. Praise You, bless You, our mighty God."

Someone present should act as leader and then lead the group in prayers of renunciation of the occult sins and prayers of forgiveness. Since an important part of successful ministry appears to be breaking the demonic heredity in the family line, we all repeat out loud the entire list. (None of us knows all that our ancestors may have been up to!) The format which we use follows:

"Thank you, Lord, for dying for my sins, for your glorious resurrection, and for making me a new creature in Christ by faith in your precious blood. Dear Lord, I have a confession to make:
I have sought supernatural experience apart from you.
I have disobeyed your Word.
I want you to help me renounce all these things and cleanse me in body, soul, and spirit in Jesus' name.
I renounce witchcraft and magic, both black and white.
I renounce ouija boards and all other occult games.
I renounce all seances, clairvoyance, and mediums; ESP, second sight, and mind-reading.
I renounce all fortune telling, palm reading, tea-leaf reading, crystal balls, Tarot and other card laying.
I renounce all astrology and interest in horoscopes.
I renounce the heresy of reincarnation and all healing groups involved in metaphysics.

I renounce all hypnosis under any excuse or authority.

I break any curse placed on me from any occult source, in Jesus' name.

I renounce all curiosity about either future or past, and which is outside Thy will.

I renounce water witching or dowsing, levitation, body lifting, table tipping, psychometry, and automatic writing.

I renounce astral projection and other demonic skills.

I renounce all literature I have ever read in any of these fields, and vow that I will destroy such books in my own possession.

I now break, in the name of Jesus Christ, all psychic heredity, and any demonic hold upon my family line as a result of the disobedience of any of my ancestors. I also break any bonds of physical or mental illness, in Jesus' name.

I also break all demonic subjection to my mother, father, grandparents, or any other human being.

In the name of Jesus Christ I renounce everything psychic and occult.

I renounce every cult that denies the blood of Christ.

I renounce every philosophy that denies the divinity of Christ.

I call upon the Lord to set me free.

Lord, I have another confession to make. I have not loved, but have resented certain people.

I call upon You, Lord, to help me forgive them.
I do now forgive ....
(Here we pause for several minutes while each person puts the names in there which the Lord brings to mind, either of persons living or dead.)
I do now forgive myself.
I renounce every evil spirit that binds or torments me and I call upon the Lord to set me free."

The above list is a frank copy of some actual prayers used by our friend, Don Basham; some which appear in my other book, and some new ones which we have discovered in recent months and weeks to be especially important for some people. The Word of God warns in Ephesians 4:27 that we are to "give no opportunity to the devil." These prayers of preparation remove the ground or opportunity which demons have had for attacking us and make the ministry of casting out spirits far more certain of success. In a certain sense, the devil is a legalist; he knows his rights and will hold on as long as he can present any case against us, based on disobedience to the Word of God.

Once the group has affirmed these prayers and renunciations aloud, the leader of the group may then come against Satan and the demons in some such verbal attack as the following: "In the name and authority of the Lord Jesus Christ, I come against you, Satan, and all demons tormenting all persons present. I command you to name yourselves and come out, in Jesus' name, ruler spirits first."

An entire chapter will follow on the ruler demons; suffice it to say here that it is helpful if the "big fellows" are located and gotten rid of first. Seldom does a person have only one demon spirit. They are found in gangs in much the same way as the underworld of crime operates; their success depends upon the control of a strong man or big bully which has been devastating the life, often without the victim being aware of the existence of such a one.

Reactions in the bodies of those tormented should follow the general command against the spirits: headaches, nausea, shaking, fainting, stomach pain, and so on. When such manifestations occur, command the spirit *within that person* to name itself. Sometimes it is wise to make it clear that you are not speaking to the person, in such a way as this: "I am speaking to the demon and not the person: give me your name, spirit now manifesting, in Jesus' name I command you."

Occasionally the demon will speak right out of the person in a harsh voice of its own. More often a word is powerfully suggested to the mind of the individual. If no word comes to the tormented one, we have found the Lord is faithful in revealing its identity to others in the group through the gift of discerning of spirits mentioned in the last chapter.

Once the spirit is named, we ask the whole group to renounce or pit their human wills against it, like this: "I renounce the spirit of *hate* (or whatever has been named) in the name of Jesus Christ."

Then it is a simple matter to say, "spirit of *hate*, we command you to come out of him in

Jesus' name." Continue the commands for a few minutes if necessary, or sing songs about the blood of Christ. Quoting Scripture that counters the specific sin represented by the spirit is also found to be most effective. (A list of such Scriptures is found in the appendix at the back of this book.) General verses that help often in deliverance services are Revelation 12:11, Luke 10:19, James 4:7, and Galatians 5:22, 23.

When the demon leaves, the person usually will sense some release, (often through the mouth) with coughing, sighs, sobs, or burping. Sometimes there will be screams such as those recorded in Acts 8 under the ministry of Philip. Usually there is more than one demon within a person. Therefore the feeling of release upon expulsion of a spirit is often short-lived, and new negative experiences by the tormented person follow in a few moments. For this reason, we find it helpful to address the next spirit somewhat like this: "Spirit now manifesting, next one in line, give us your name."

The same process is followed for each spirit until a clear indication is given the group that the time of ministry should end. Frequently it is simply the testimony of the person being delivered who testifies to being free and feeling better. However, often it is through a word of wisdom given to those ministering that the person has endured enough; probably the spirits already cast out are all the person is able to stand against in the days ahead. More may come out later. These the person may either cast out of himself or have friends cast out of him. The important thing to realize is that the Lord is the Deliverer, and He alone knows the hearts of all of us. He is the One who must direct the deliverance process, and He knows how much any of us are able to bear.

There is a whole chapter in Don Basham's book, *Deliver Us From Evil*, on self-deliverance, as well as a directory of places where deliverance is ministered. Both that book and *OUT! In the Name of Jesus* have many detailed examples of deliverances. We urge the reader to study both of these for further enlightenment on this subject. Detailed discussions of individual exorcisms are beyond the scope of this brief summary.

However, we should answer the frequently asked question, "Why not cast them out all at once, as Christ did the Legion?" The most obvious fact here is that the Lord Jesus Christ did a number of things in His earthly ministry which have not yet been done by members of His body, such as being transfigured before the disciples. Some day He may give us more power. Now we rejoice in what He sees fit to do as spirits are cast out one by one. For those who doubt whether this is necessary, we can only reply that many people who come to our Friday night meetings have earlier tried the "quick convention method" and have remained in their torment. Praise God that He *does* want us to be free, and will see us through to that point, by whatever means He chooses to use!

7 | Wrestling Against Rulers

One of the great blessings of the New American Standard Bible is its great clarity, accuracy, and consistency in translating words in the original languages the same way each time. Because of this policy of the scholars, some truths have emerged quite prominently which Satan and his hosts have done their level best to keep from the Church. One of these truths is that there are ruler spirits which are our first and most formidable enemies in spiritual warfare. "For our struggle is not against flesh and blood, but *against the rulers*, against the powers, against the world-forces of this darkness, against the spiritual forces of wickedness in the heavenly places." (Ephesians 6:12)

In the contemporary deliverance ministry we are finding that the ruler spirits must be identified, cast out and stood against, if a person hopes to remain free of demonic oppression. These spirits have exactly the opposite qualities to the fruit of the Holy Spirit listed in Galatians 5:22, 23. Usually a tormented person is bound by one ruler spirit, although he may also have other ruler spirits. For example, a person bound by a spirit of *pride* as the ruler spirit can conceivably have all the others we often find as rulers: *self-pity, hate, lust, fear, rebellion*, and *un-*

belief. However, the big problem in that person's life will be pride, and this will be the thing he will have to stand against most consistently. In other words, many of his most subtle temptations after deliverance from the spirit of *pride* will be opportunities for proud behavior and actions.

In order to locate which spirit is ruler, we in the New Testament Fellowship use the methods outlined in chapter six. Then after the person's deliverance from that demon, we urge him to memorize verses which are effective in standing against it. A list of these for each of the demons we have found to be rulers is found in the appendix of this book.

Perhaps examples will help to show how important this matter is. During the past three years we have seen people delivered from ruler spirits, some of whom have stood in victory afterwards, and some not. We must present both success and failure stories if we are going to be true to the facts and heed the Lord's warning of Matthew 12:43-45.

A young woman had been miraculously healed of a terrible disease. She had a sparkling testimony in most areas of her life, but often wept before the Lord in secret because of a problem she could share with no one: she hated her own children. When she heard teaching about deliverance and the ruler spirits, she realized *hate* had bound her all her life. She renounced it, cast it out of herself, and was set free.

A young teenager became quite disturbed and ran away from home. When the heartbroken parents got her back, they brought her to our Fellowship for ministry. The key spirit in her case proved to be *rebellion*. Until she would agree to submit to her parents, there was no release. As soon as she yielded, verbalizing it in the practical way of agreeing to go back to school, the demon *rebellion* (which she had renounced an hour earlier) left her. She is a happy, normal young person today.

A mental patient came for help some years ago. We cast demons out of her, all of which apparently returned very soon. Recently a visiting speaker in the area spoke on deliverance, and this girl again decided she wanted to be free. Terry started coming out of our regular prayer meetings, but our approach with her this time was different. Having learned in the interim about the ruler spirits, we made it our primary business the first night she came to locate that one. It was revealed to us through discerning of spirits as *pride*. Because of its great hold on Terry, she had come under many religious delusions. She has also been a compulsive talker—a problem often associated with a great need for deliverance.

After we cast out that spirit, we instructed Terry to "study to be quiet" (I Thess. 4:11) and learn to listen. We urged her to carry a little notebook with her and write down what people tell her so that she may check at the end of a day whether she has really been listening or not. On days when she listens to others, reads and memorizes the Word of God, and fulfills her daily chores, she has victory. When she slips back into the old pattern of constant talk and an unteachable attitude, she has failure.

Over the months she is making progress, however. She has just those spirits cast out that she can stand against, and casts out some herself when she feels strong enough. We are believing God for the full transformation of this girl in time as fleshly pride gives way to true humility. This case will serve to help those who think of the deliverance ministry as an "easy out" for people who do not want to face their problems in the flesh. It is no such thing! Deliverance from evil spirits removes the supernatural part of the problem, so that the person is able to deal with the natural one.

Once my husband and I ministered to a man who was terribly bound by the spirit of *self-pity*. Although it did not repond to the command to name itself, its name was given to us through discerning of spirits. Once we challenged it and had Frank renounce it, it began manifesting in a very dramatic way. The man began to moan and writhe, while the spirit spoke out of him in an entirely different voice with a foreign accent, using terrible grammar. (This fact was most striking, for the man himself has an excellent command of English and is a native-born American.) We finally cast it out and several others, each of them manifesting itself in a dramatic way. We warned him that *self-pity* was his basic problem and that he must guard against it.

It was soon apparent that the spirit had come back, and Frank was more tormented than ever. His pattern of behavior since then has been to follow courses of action in which he will be forced to feel sorry for himself. In other words, the spirit of *self-pity* evidently motivates much of his behavior, which in turn gives him an excuse to be miserable.

Once recently we were praying with a couple

of powerful intercessors who mentioned having a burden for this man. As they prayed, one woman said the Lord revealed that Frank had given ground to the enemy in his life by believing a false prophecy said over him personally some years before.

This case brings up an important point. Personal prophesying over details of people's individual lives is often divination or fortune telling, not divine prophecy at all. It is to be avoided and groups which practise it should be warned that they are treading on very dangerous ground. The author knows of two instances of this which brought heartbreak into lives and set back untold numbers of observers in their spiritual growth.

Once at a convention a prominent speaker was asked by a pregnant woman whether her child would be a boy or a girl. The speaker said it would be a boy; it was a girl. However, that is far from the end of the story. Many heard of it and were disillusioned with both the speaker and the spiritual movement in that area. The couple themselves have suffered from severe demonic oppression since.

On another occasion a godly woman approached another whose husband was unsaved, giving her the happy "prophecy" that the unconverted husband would attend the next charismatic convention with his wife. The woman believed the statement and made plans to attend the next convention. Despite all maneuvers to try to get him to go, the husband refused. For a long time the wife was bitter and upset, although she did go to the convention alone.

The sequel to this story is interesting. The

would-be prophet found it impossible to get free from an affliction for which she had much prayer until the spirit of *pride* was cast out—responsible for all this havoc. She will stay free from the affliction only as she stays free of pride, if other cases we have observed teach us anything. The Lord Jesus Christ is still saying, "Go, and sin no more," to those who come to Him for healing and deliverance.

On one ignominious day, someone actually prophesied "over a young unmarried couple at one of our New Testament Fellowship meetings that they would marry and serve the Lord together. Fortunately this unwise comment was heard by several of our elders who judged it to be spurious and told the "prophet" so. One elder went to the young couple at once and urged them to ignore the whole thing, advising them that God would show each of them in His time what His will was for their lives and relationship.

It is well for people who have allowed themselves to be used by the enemy in this way to confess all such matters to the Lord as sin. Then we have also found it helpful for them to take the ground back from Satan which they gave him in such incidents. A good way to do this is simply to address a command directly to Satan, such as: "Satan ,in the name of Jesus Christ I take back all the ground I gave you in my life when I gave a false prophecy to————or believed one said over me on these occasions:————." Since I myself was bound by a *lying spirit of prophecy* and had no small difficulty getting free, the Lord has given me special compassion for those so bound. Words of encouragement are in order. If one can humble himself under God and submit to the objective judgment of his mature Christian brethren about such matters, he can be set completely free.

There are no lone rangers in the Christian faith. We are meant to function as a body made up of many different members, and it is this interdependence which is our greatest safeguard against the spiritual deceptions of the evil one. Those seeking to be free must humbly accept the evaluation of freinds who are kind enough to give us insight we may lack ourselves. One very dear friend of mine talked with me on the phone one day and frankly assessed my comments this way: "That sounds like self-pity to me!" As soon as I got off the phone, I told the Lord I was sorry and confessed this as sin. I also renounced the spirit and commanded it to leave again, in case it was also back. Thank God for friends who can be honest with us and give us light when we have none ourselves. Perhaps no state is more dangerous than that which resists help or criticism. The subtle nature of our battle, especially against the ruler spirits, requires humility and a teachable spirit.

Vivian is a young woman who had exactly the opposite problem to the ones mentioned earlier in the chapter. As a new believer she actually had a vision of the Lord Himself and from that time on an extremely close walk with Him. Not only did He endow her with a number of spiritual gifts, but also He gave her considerable direct guidance. Not once did anything revealed to her during this period of real closeness to Him contradict itself, and the fruit of actions based on her guidance was excellent—both in her own life and others.

However, in one meeting Vivian heard a woman prophesy who evidently was under the influence of demon spirits. This experience so troubled Vivian that she began to discount her own genuine experience. Before long there was a great silence between her and God. Although she read the Word faithfully, she got no more specific direction for her life.

As she told me her story, the Spirit of God impressed upon my mind that a spirit of *unbelief* had gained a hold on her life because of her wrong interpretation of her own experience after hearing the disturbed woman prophesy. When I shared this with her, she renounced the spirit of *unbelief*, took the ground back she had given Satan for not believing God, and confessed the sin of unbelief to the Lord. We cast the spirit out and she cried with great relief as it went. Soon afterward she reported that the peace she knew in her former close walk with the Lord Jesus had returned.

This account will point up the fact that there is much genuine supernatural divine guidance and revelation today, which is why Satan is trying to discredit it by counterfeiting. Unless there is a real article, there are no counterfeits of it. The very presence of the counterfeits emphasizes the existence of the real thing.

How do we judge supernatural gifts, ministries, and guidance? It seems to me that there are three primary ways. 1) Are they scriptural? God never contradicts Himself; all guidance or power truly from Him confirms His written Word and is confirmed by it. 2) What is the fruit of them, both in the life of the one ministering and of those being ministered unto? If havoc, chaos, deteriorating or wrong relationships result from such ministry, it must have an evil source. If, on the other hand, "love, joy, peace, patience, kindness, goodness, faithfulness, gentleness and self control" result from such ministry, it must have originated with God. 3) Is Jesus Christ lifted up and exalted from the ministry being judged? Here is the third "acid test" for such ministry. If anyone other than the Lord Jesus Christ is being magnified there must be a "check" registered within us.

The apparent aim of the ruler demons is to impress those we meet with their characteristics rather than those of the Spirit of God. As a person comes under a greater and greater degree of control by such a spirit, God's Spirit will be more and more grieved and less evident in that life. Thus it is imperative that the evil presences be recognized and stopped.

A basic rule of warfare is that we identify and locate the enemy. Had not India countered the slaughter of the Bengali people by defeating the west Pakistan army, even more than three million would have been murdered during the bloody birth of Bangladesh. It was no good pretending that there were no malicious, merciless enemies, for every day they did more harm.

Just so in the spiritual warfare. It will not do for the Church of Jesus Christ to ignore the enemies in the camp any longer. A steady stream of refugees (ten million of them in ten months) showed India and the world that there was a problem in Bangladesh demanding solution. Today a steady stream of backsliders, professing to be Christians but fleeing from the battle, prove powerfully the existence of a fifth column working within the body of Christ which must be expelled.

If we ignore this truth, we do so at great peril. Some years ago when we were first learning about spiritual warfare, a tormented friend called for help. We suggested he contact the only charismatic church we knew of at that time, for we had heard they had a deliverance ministry. Sam went to these people and they asked him how he felt. When he said confused, they cast a spirit of confusion out of him. When he said depressed, they cast a spirit of depression out of him. He felt better and left, but within days was much worse off. He and his family discounted the deliverance ministry from that time on and sought medical help.

Once Sam sought my counsel and asked me what I thought was wrong with him. I told him I believed he was oppressed by evil spirits and had given up too easily after just one brief time of ministry. He answered me that he could not believe his trouble was caused by evil spirits; he could just never believe that.

At that time I knew nothing of spirits confessing themselves in conversation nor did I know of ruler demons. Later, with the insight of several years' experience, I realized God was allowing me to hear a ruler spirit of *unbelief* confess itself over and over in that otherwise futile conversation. We wrote and asked Sam to come for help, but neither he nor his wife believed we had any answers for them.

Not long ago Sam committed suicide.

What will it take to wake us up to the fact

that we must wrestle against these rulers, as the apostle Paul said? May God open eyes and bring repentance to thousands of readers before it is too late. After all, He is the Deliverer! Think how the great bondage of His own people must grieve Him. Today He is saying to His Church as He said to Moses:

> "I have surely seen the affliction of My people who are in Egypt, and have given heed to their cry because of their taskmasters, for I am aware of their sufferings. So I have come down to deliver them . . ." (Exodus 3: 7, 8)

8 | Keeping Your Deliverance

As I have pointed out through the whole of this book, deliverance is God's provision to set us free from the inroads that Satan and his demons have made in our lives. Once we have been delivered, we must determine to remain free. Just as in the salvation experience, man must decide with his own will to turn his life over to God and then trust God to make this decision a reality, so, after deliverance, man must decide to remain free and then trust God to supply the power and self-control that are necessary to keep his freedom.

There are two keys to keeping our deliverance: we must abide in Christ, and we must resist Satan. The word *abide* is briefly summarized by the first half of James 4:7, "Submit therefore to God." Without crowning Jesus Lord of our lives and submitting fully to Him, there can be no abiding in His presence; no love, joy and peace; and certainly no permanent deliverance from evil powers.

Jesus said, "If you abide in Me, and My words abide in you, ask whatever you wish, and it shall be done for you" (John 15:7). Moses said, "Lord, Thou hast been our dwelling place in all generations" (Psalm 90:1). Another psalmist said, "He who dwells in the shelter of the Most

High will abide in the shadow of the Almighty" (Psalm 91:1). Where we live, in our innermost being, determines our victory as Christians.

Once we submit to God, we are ready for the second command in James 4:7: "Resist the devil and he will flee from you." For some strange reason (known best by our cunning deceiver) contemporary Christians often regard that sentence this way: "Ignore the devil and he will flee from you." By some it is considered a mark of spirituality never to mention Satan or his demons. Many cling to the notion that if they just leave Satan alone, he will leave them alone. Nothing could be further from the truth, as the defeated lives of the believers who argue this way so often show. Ephesians 6:10-18 should be memorized and written on the hearts of every believer. We are to *stand* on the Lord's side against Satan and every attempt of his minions to oppress us again. The remaining part of this chapter will be divided into five areas that will help you to keep your deliverance by abiding in Christ and resisting Satan.

1. Bring Your Life Into Scriptural Order:

The Scriptures teach that only those who are willing to make Jesus Lord of their lives can also claim Him as Saviour (Matthew 7:21-27; John 15). A young married woman called me one night complaining bitterly that her life had never changed after she accepted Christ as her Saviour. Betty had married an unbeliever and found that things had gone from bad to worse. There was profanity, quarreling, and a total lack of discipline or even routine in their home. She and her preschool children slept everyday until noon. Could she come for deliverance?

Simply, but methodically I told Betty she needed to commit her life to Jesus as *Lord*: to declare Him "Boss" over her entire life and get herself and her children in to a disciplined life for His sake. I outlined the practical steps of bringing one's life into order which follow in this chapter, and told her that after following them, she would be a candidate for deliverance.

A month later Betty called again, her life and home in order, her voice calm and assured, and her conversation filled with Jesus—who had indeed changed her life. She still wanted deliverance from torment, for which she was now quite ready. Of course we agreed to help her, and she came right away even though—a blinding snowstorm raged outside.

Betty's life became so radiant following her deliverance and baptism in the Holy Spirit on that snowy day, that she has been used to influence a wide circle with her light. Soon a lifetime friend, Kitty, came to the Lord; her life was equally transformed. Both young women attend the spiritual retreats we hold in this area monthly, and both have seen their husbands come to the Lord within this past month.

Many people do not see the importance of having one's life in order scripturally. But, unless one's life proves that a person is living the Word of God, Satan has a right to question whether Jesus is Lord. We always try to explain to people this whole matter of standing against the demons once they are cast out. You see, the demons look for a place to come back as Scripture says in Luke 11:24. "When the unclean spirit goes out of a man, it passes through waterless places seeking rest, and not finding any, it says, 'I will return to my house from which I came.' And when it comes, it finds it swept and put in order. Then it goes and takes along seven other spirits more evil than itself, and they go in and live there; and the last state of that man becomes worse than the first." Lack of Scriptural order in a life is the 'for rent sign' that shows that a house is empty and God's Spirit and His Word have not filled the vacated places in that life. This person is in danger of being worse off than he was before deliverance. Dick and I feel that it is dishonest to minister deliverance under such conditions.

2. Be Filled By The Holy Spirit:

We feel that it is absolutely essential for a believer to be filled by the Holy Spirit if he is to have a fighting chance against Satan. When the believer is infilled by the Holy Spirit, he is empowered to use his spiritual authority. This is not an optional dessert in the Christian diet, but it is the bread and meat of our life in God. And, though a person may say he has received the baptism in the Holy Spirit, this is not the end of the story. The Greek tense used in Ephesians 5:18 is the continuing present tense. This could accurately be translated *"be being filled* with the Holy Spirit." We see that not just a one-time experience is commanded but a daily walk in the Spirit.

One of the first evidences of the filling of the Holy Spirit comes as a believer dedicates his life more and more to the will of God and the Holy

Spirit in him. He will find certain help and strength from God that will enable him to resist Satan. We find that it is the Lord's strength, not ours, that helps us to stand firm against the lies and schemes of the devil. It helps greatly to begin every day by a statement of intention to do God's will and then to follow through on it. Stella (Chapter Six) starts her day by saying, "I *will* read three chapters of the Word. I *will* learn a verse today. I *will* witness to my unsaved neighbor in the hospital. I *will not* feel sorry for myself today." In this way, she puts her human will (empowered by the Holy Spirit) against the will of the demons. Victory is assured, even though there may be a battle before it is won.

At Columbia Bible College, where Dick and I trained for missionary service, Frank Sells taught thousands the secret of victory in living the Christian life with this simple diagram:

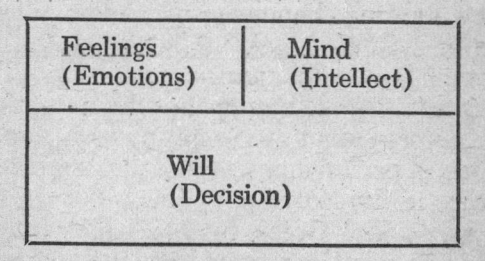

Feelings (Emotions)	Mind (Intellect)
Will (Decision)	

When the foundation is right, the rest of the structure will eventually be built in order above it. Making the right decision governs the right outcome. Salvation and a life of victory are both a matter of the will. My feelings or my mental arguments may cry against what God says, but if I trust Him and decide His way, everything will turn out all right. On the other hand, impulses that are followed solely on the basis of emotional experience or a well reasoned argument may never reach the will at all. No matter how God's Word reaches us initially, it must get down into our *wills* in order to change our lives.

We have seldom seen anyone delivered from nicotine who did not first say, "I will never smoke another cigarette." Similar strong affirmations (all of which involve the human will) must be made by a drug addict, an alcoholic, or a homosexual who desires to be freed. Our words are more powerful than we realize, as Mark 11:23 clearly indicates. Those who confess victory in Jesus' name are entitled to it, for they are on God's side, and He will use His mighty resources to see them through. Those who confess defeat will also have defeat. So again I emphasize, through the Lord's strength we can stand firm in victory.

The second evidence of the infilling of the Holy Spirit will come to the believer as he sees God's kind of love, Calvary love, evidenced in his own life. In ancient Greek, this type of love is referred to as *agape* or divine, self-giving love.

God's *agape* love asks nothing about the worth of the one loved, but only reveals the character and grace of the one who loves. God loves because He cannot help it; it is His nature to love.

In I John 4:16b, we learn that "God is love, and the one who abides in love abides in God, and God abides in him." Moreover, to love is a *command*, not merely a nice idea (Matthew 22:37-39). Only when we love Christ with a passion that eclipses every other love will we find that we can love others His way. In fact, our love for one another is simply the proof that we really belong to Jesus Christ: "We know that we have passed out of death into life, because we love the brethren. He who does not love abides in death" (I John 3:14). Is it any wonder that "We love, because He first loved us?" (I John 4:19).

A third evidence of the infilling of the Holy Spirit in a believer's life is that he becomes a "doer" of the word, not just a "hearer". Those who put God's Word into practice in their lives are earmarked for God's continuing blessing in their lives (James 1:22). God gives us light from His Word in order that we may walk in it. Light received and applied will mean more light given; light rejected will result in less light afterwards. Walking in the light is God's great condition for close fellowship with others and for the cleansing of His blood upon us for all our sins (I John 1:7). We can expect neither fellowship with Him nor cleansing by Him if we disobey.

Balance is the fourth mark of a Spirit-filled believer. Balance shows the self-control and discipline of the Holy Spirit in a life (Galatians 5:22, 23; II Timothy 1:7). Great variations in behavior and mood should not be tolerated in the mature Christian experience. A Christian who allows his decisions to be made on the basis of his feelings will be sharply limited in his usefulness to the kingdom of God, since "we walk by faith, not by sight" (II Corinthians 5:7). The sooner one finds that he has been saved to serve, the more profitable he is. "Therefore, my beloved brethren, be steadfast, unmovable, always abounding in the work of the Lord, knowing that your toil is not in vain in the Lord" (I Corinthians 15:58).

Fifth, a person who is truly walking in the Spirit will find that he delights in his Lord—gives praise to God (Psalm 37:4). Learning to lift the hands in praise (Psalm 63:4) and surrender (Psalm 119:48) and to bless the Lord at all times (Psalm 34:1 and II Thessalonians 5:18) are two of the church's great discoveries in today's outpouring of the Holy Spirit. God tells us in 1 Thessalonians 5:16-18, "Rejoice always; pray without ceasing; in everything give thanks; for this is God's will for you in Christ Jesus." There is power in praise, and we find that a praising Christian is well on the way to continual victory over Satan's attacks.

Singing in the Spirit is perhaps the most delightful way to find release in praise. Either in English or in the tongues we can lift our voices to God in song. Sometimes we use familar tunes; often God gives fresh, new melodies, especially for important scripture verses.

A while back, in my private times of singing in the Spirit at the piano, the same tune and words in my prayer language kept coming. I mentioned this casually to Dave and Judy Brown, who have a coffeehouse ministry in Schenectady called "Snoopy's Place." Judy asked me to play and sing in her presence, and took out her notebook. Soon the Lord gave her the interpretation: one verse that night, and two verses ten days later. The message is a prophetic word to all of Christ's own, calling them to a banquet of full fellowship with Him. Heeding its message will prepare us for the great wedding feast which is coming when the heavenly Bridegroom returns for His bride, the Church. Because of the victorious invitation given in this song, and because of the joy that we have singing it in prayer groups in my area, I am including it at the end of the book. May it bless many of your prayer groups as it has ours, and may it be the start of many Spirit-given songs that you will sing in your times of praise.

3. Maintain Communication With God:

If we are to keep our eyes on Jesus, if we are to abide in Christ, then one of our most important duties is to keep in continual communication with God. God knew our need for communication with Him from the beginning of time. We can be sure that He will go far to keep us walking in His way as we sincerely desire to do so.

For this reason, He gave us the Bible. It is His Word, His guidance, His way. It reveals His heart and His mind. It records His working in the lives of men from the beginning of history. The Word of God is truth. It is our main source of strength against Satan. It must be read systematically, believed, and memorized, and then applied to displace Satan's lies. Scripture is called "the sword of the Spirit," and Jesus used it as His only weapon against Satan in the wilderness temptation. Jesus answered each of the devil's temptations with statements prefaced with the words, "it is written ... it is written ... it is written." Then He commanded Satan to depart.

In 1959 I discovered an effective plan for daily scripture reading through the teaching of Roy Gustafson, who shared his own method. I have been using it ever since and find that in this manner I can get through the Bible once a year or at least every 15 months.

Very simply, the plan divides the Bible into six sections which I read on six week days. Monday's reading is from the Pentateuch (Genesis to Deuteronomy), Tuesday's from the historical books (Joshua to Esther), Wednesday's from the poetic books (Job to Song of Solomon), Thursday's from the prophets (Isaiah to Malachi), Friday's from the Gospels (Matthew to John), and Saturday's from the rest of the New Testament.

The schedule works like this: each day at least three chapters are read from the assigned section, the stopping place marked by a penciled date at the end of the passage. For example, if we read Genesis 1-3 on Monday, we mark the date at the end of chapter 3. Then the following Monday we erase last week's date and begin reading at chapter 4. The same procedure will be followed on Joshua on Tuesday, Job on Wednesday, etc. The advantages of the date markings are many, including a gentle rebuke for negligence when the date is two or three weeks old!

Mercifully, the human mind cannot think two thoughts at once. When oppressive thoughts come, we are to displace them with appropriate scripture verses (II Corinthians 10:3-5). Even if we must repeat these verses many, many times, it is surely worth the effort in order to be completely free.

Of course, equally important in our communication with God is our personal meditation, our time of private communion and prayer with the One that we serve. As you study the lives of the men and women who have been used greatly by God, you'll find without fail that each was convinced of the need of prayer. In almost every case, these saints began each day with an hour or more of seeking God's face. It seems wise for each individual to seek God's will as to the time and place most appropriate in his life for daily prayer. As a person grows in Christ, he will find the Spirit leading him more and more into fuller and deeper prayer times.

One should remember that there are many different types of prayer, and that in your personal meditation you can combine all of these types. A person can spend time simply praising God. Again, he may find that he has many needs that he wants to present to the Lord for himself and for others. The prayer of petition is certainly in order at this time. Praying in the Spirit, that is in tongues, speaks secrets to the heart of God while the believer is edified and built up in his faith.

The interesting thing that many Christians seem to forget, is that communication is a two-way street. As we pray we should always be ready to receive God's answer. Therefore, quiet times of waiting and listening should be a part of our personal meditation. God will speak to the heart of the believer if we will give Him a chance. These times of comfort, instruction and love should become part of the life-blood that flows daily into the believer's life.

I keep a precious little notebook of prophetic words, and I urge all of God's children to maintain such a notebook. God will speak very gently in your spirit as you ask the Lord for the bread of life for the day. It is well to seek God for His specific word to you after you have been reading His written word; then His thoughts are already dwelling in your mind. (Let me stress that there should never be a *compulsion* to write, however, for such pressure would indicate a demonic source. Not a few people these days need deliverance from a demonic spirit of automatic writing.) However, do not allow the fear of deception to keep you from truly enjoying one of God's gifts.

One day recently the Lord put these words into my spirit:

"There is a river, the reality of which none can know except those who drink from its well springs high in the mountains of suffering. Be pleased to dwell on these mountains in My presence, singing my praise, and you shall be carried on to this river.

No earthly circumstance can touch you once you are released upon its waters. No fury from hell can change its course. You are moving towards this river of My rest. Keep your eyes fixed upon Me and I will never fail you. Do not be anxious about tomorrow, for it is already bathed in the sunlight of My love—already written with the pen of My fulfillment.

Yet a little while and you shall see Me. Can you not wait for earth's little hour? The joys ahead exceed your powers to express them in mere words or imprison them with your thoughts. Trust Me to do what is right, and I will guide your footsteps to the land of eternal daylight. Shadows are spawned in hell; joy is the legacy I have given each of My children who dares to turn his back on every earthly treasure."

We must remember that all of our communication with God rests upon our voluntary acceptance of His Lordship. God will never force Himself upon us. When Eve turned her back on God and listened to the subtle, serpentine lie that she would be like God if she disobeyed Him, she let self sit on the throne of her heart. Ever since then, God has had this goal with all His children: to become King as well as Father; Lord as well as Saviour.

Since self dies hard, there is a continuing struggle within the heart of every Christian. Satan is happy to provide a host of his helpers to keep tottering self alive and perched on the throne of the human heart as long as possible. The proper strategy is to admit that we are unable to live the Christian life by ourselves. Then we bow down to our victorious Lord and invite His Holy Spirit to reign supreme from within our hearts.

If we allow the Spirit to reveal Christ within us, we will learn to accept with joy the "nails" He uses to crucify our flesh. God can then use painful circumstances or difficult relationships to pierce quite effectively our self-centeredness. Jesus said, "if anyone wishes to come after Me, let him deny himself, and take up his cross daily, and follow Me. For whoever wishes to save his life shall lose it, but whoever loses his life for My sake, he is the one who will save it" (Luke 9:23-24).

What is this cross? It is the life of *voluntary* self-denial. We live as disciples of our Lord, who had no place to lay His head. For some this means a life which includes loneliness, physical privation, and travel in order to carry the Gospel to those who have never heard. For others it means staying in a difficult marriage or place of service so that God may get the glory from a life of obedience and His word might be honored. For still others it means facing the misunderstanding and rejection of those held most dear because we refuse to compromise the truth.

Bearing one's cross means simply that we no longer do our own will, but the will of the One who has sent us. Yet the strange mystery is this: the more fully we accept His will, the more real His presence becomes in our lives. One young woman, Donna, had a real battle with passivity of the mind after the expulsion of the spirit of *unbelief*. Depression, even suicidal thoughts bothered her during times when she did not make the effort to keep her mind active. Finally the Holy Spirit helped her to see that she had been a sponge for Scripture rather than a channel. Her practice had been to take and take under preaching and teaching ministries. Now she determined to give others the Word of God, and began finding opportunities with friends and neighbors to sit down with the Bible over a cup of coffee. She was amazed to find how God used her once this change took place in her life. And as an interesting by-product of her sharing, she noticed the yo-yo moods were less frequent and were not as extreme. Out of her former suffering emerged a rapidly maturing believer experiencing more of the presence of God in her life.

So it becomes evident that our growth and

our communication with God is directly related to our willingness to give up our right to our own way in our lives. God will communicate, will guide, will teach, will reveal His Word to those who voluntarily seek His will.

4. Put on The Armor Of God:

The *armor* of God is the secret of victory both in defensive and offensive warfare with Satan. Our *righteousness* is not our own, but Christ's righteousness with which He clothes us (I Corinthians 1:30). *Salvation* is nothing we have done for ourselves, but a gift Jesus bought with His own blood (Ephesians 2:8-9; Titus 3:5; I Peter 1:18-21). When Satan tempts or accuses us and we feel we will never make it, we turn the battle over to the Lord Jesus, saying, "Jesus, *You* are my strength, my goodness in this situation."

Our feet wear *Gospel shoes* (Ephesians 6:15)—a perfect fit for people who want to remain free from demonic oppression. We ought to be sharing Jesus with people wherever we go. It is almost impossible to complain, criticize, or resent people if our conversation is centered on the Lord Jesus.

Faith, as our shield (Ephesians 6:16; I Peter 1:5), is held out against every attack of the enemy as the attacks come. Satan's lies bounce off God's promises when those promises are calmly stated and firmly believed. In 1967 and '68 I was often rudely awakened in the middle of the night by something which said to me, "You are going to hell; you're going to hell." Commanding the enemy to depart in Jesus' Name, I would slip into the bathroom where I could use the light and not awaken the family. There I learned many Bible verses and repeated them over and over again until they were written on my heart. In time, the demon saw that I meant business and the attacks ceased. By doing this I was using the *sword of the Spirit*, the Word of God. This is also using the Truth—the Word of God, and in Ephesians 6 we find that the *girdle of truth* is another part of our armor.

Without this armor of God, we find ourselves defenseless against Satan. It is important that the believer put on the armor of God each day by faith and that he walk by faith in the protection of God throughout the day.

5. Be Honest About Your Own Deliverance:

In order to keep one's deliverance, it is most important that a person be totally honest about it. Though we may feel embarrassed or may even be ashamed of some of the inroads that we find in our own lives, we should remember that Satan and his demons are not a part of our personality. When we have gone through deliverance, the freedom that comes is the freedom from bondage. This freedom is to be joyfully shared with others so that God's whole message, His whole Gospel of the freedom of Christ, can be preached. You must realize that your experience may lead to another person's freedom.

In Philippians 2:7, KJV, we see that Jesus made Himself of "no reputation." We should be willing to share His ignominy on earth if we are to share His glory in heaven. Jesus told the Gadarene demoniac to go home and to tell people what great things God had done for him. Falsifying or denying the actual situation that existed in your life is simply inviting evil spirits back again. No way is so sure after deliverance as honest testimony; no path is so dangerous as deception and concealment (Revelations 12:11; Luke 9:24).

Thus we win the complete victory through Christ. Our basic decisions must line up our will with His; then He is faithful to give us the grace and power to follow through. May each of us learn to live in continual victory through Christ, that we may be fully free—a people delivered from bondage, a people who know our authority in Christ and how to use it effectively to help others to freedom.

Appendix

Effective Scripture Verses to Memorize in
Fighting Through to Victory

*General Verses
for Spiritual
Warfare*

James 4:7
Luke 10:19
Rev. 12:11
II Cor. 10:3-5
Eph. 6: 10-18
Prov. 18:10
Mark 16:17
I John 4:1-4

*Verses to Use against the
Ruler Demons*

HATE

I John 3:14
I John 4:16b &
 19-21
Psalm 60:4
Song of Sol. 2:4
Luke 10:27
Matt. 22:37-39
Prov. 10:12
I Thess. 4:8
Col. 3:12-14
II Thess. 3:5
Phil. 2:1 & 2
Eph. 3:16-19
I Cor. 13:4-8a
Gal. 5:22,23

PRIDE

Prov. 16:18, 19
Prov. 6:16-17a
Prov. 3:34
Prov. 13:10
Prov. 14:3
Prov. 15:25
Prov. 16:5
Prov. 21:23, 24
Prov. 28:9
Prov. 29:1 & 23
II Tim. 3: 1, 2
Phil. 2:5-8
James 4:10
I Peter 5:6

SELF-PITY

Nehemiah 8:10
 NASB
Phil. 4:13, 3:4
Psalm 33:1
Psalm 34:1-3
Psalm 50:23
Psalm 104:33, 34
Phil. 4:11, 13, 19
I Tim. 6:6
I Thess. 5:18

FEAR

Psalm 56:3
Psalm 46:1, 2
Psalm 107:2
II Tim. 1:7
Is. 44:2b and 3
I John 4:18
Heb. 13:6
Josh. 1:9

Fear of Man
Prov. 29:25
Josh. 1:5
Josh. 10:8

REBELLION

Prov. 17:11
I Sam. 15:23
Jer. 28:16
Jer. 29:32
II Tim. 3:1, 2
Eph. 5:21
Phil. 2:5-8
Phil. 2:14
I Thess. 5:18
Romans 12:1, 2
Romans 13:1, 2

		Passages to Study
LUST	*UNBELIEF*	*on Related Subjects*

II Tim. 2:22	Mark 11:23, 24	Fasting: Isaiah 58;
I Cor. 6:9, 10	Luke 1:45	Matt. 6:16-18
I Cor. 6:17-20	John 8:31, 32	Praise: II Chron. 20;
I Cor. 3:16, 17	John 7:38	Psalms 134-150
Eph. 5:3	John 6:29	Revelation 4 & 5
Lev. 19:2	Acts 27:25	Scripture: Psalm
Heb. 12:14	Heb. 11:1	119; John 8:31, 32
I Peter 2:11	I Peter 1:6, 7	Deut. 4:1,2; Rev.
Isaiah 52:11	Gal. 2:20	22:18, 19
Heb. 13:4	Mark 16: 17, 18	The Blood of Christ:
Matt. 5:27, 28		Exodus 12;
& 5:8		Hebrews 9 & 10;
Titus 1:15		Rev. 5:9,10; Rev.
		12:11

Will You Come With Me?

1. Oh, lift your eyes up, and see Me com-ing; You'll see Me com-ing, ye pure in heart. I am the light of lights, the love of all-loves, You have but tasted Me,— the best is yet to be. Look! see the table now,— is be-ing set for thee; Oh will you

2. O-pen your ears to Me, and hear Me speak-ing; You'll hear Me speak-ing to you, My child. I am the Word of Life, You'll never hun-ger; If you but taste My bread, you will be satisfied. Oh, listen! Hear My call; the meal's pre-pared for you. Oh will you

3. Oh, lift your hands up, and feel My Pre-sence; You'll feel My Pre-sence as you give thanks. You will be filled with joy,— you will drink of My love.— You have but touched Me,— but I want more of thee. Feel you be-long to Me;— will you give Me your voice? Oh will you

122

(1) come with Me, — or turn a—way?
(2) eat with Me, — or turn a—way?
Refrain: (3) sing my praise, or turn a—way?

The guest list is al-ready written; I await the reply of all who have been invited? Those who heed My call. Do you hear your name? Do you walk in love? oh, will you come with me, to the ban—quet? — Look up for I am here, Jesus, your Lord.

D.C.

WILL YOU COME WITH ME?

1. Oh, lift your eyes up and see Me coming,
   You'll see me coming, ye pure in heart.
   I am the light of lights, the love of all loves,
   You have but tasted Me, the best is yet to be.
   Look! See the table now is being set for thee.
   Oh will you come with Me, or turn away?

(Refrain)
The guest list is already written;
I await the reply of all.
Who have been invited?
Those who heed My call!
Do you hear your name?
Do you walk in love?
Oh, will you come with Me, come to the banquet?
Look up for I am here, Jesus your Lord.

2. Open your ears to Me, and hear Me speaking;
   You'll hear Me speaking to you, My child.
   I am the Word of Life. You'll never hunger;
   If you but taste My bread, you will be satisfied.
   Oh listen! Hear my call; the meal's prepared for you.
   Oh will you eat with Me, or turn away? (refrain)

3. Oh, lift your hands up, and feel My presence;
   You'll feel My presence as you give thanks.
   You will be filled with joy; you will drink of My love.
   You have but touched Me, but I want more of thee.
   Feel you belong to Me; will you give Me your voice?
   O, will you sing My praise, or turn away? (refrain)

Bibliography

Basham, Don
  Can a Christian Have a Demon? Whitaker Books, Monroeville, Pennsylvania, 1971.
  Deliver Us From Evil. Chosen Books, New York, New York, 1972.
  Handbook of Holy Spirit Baptism. Whitaker House, Monroeville, Pennsylvania, 5th Ed., 1972.
  Handbook of Tongues, Interpretation, & Prophecy. Whitaker House, Monroeville, Pennsylvania, 1971.

Brooks, Pat
  Climb Mount Moriah. Whitaker House, Monroeville, Pennsylvania, 1974.
  OUT! In the Name of Jesus. Creation House, Carol Stream, Illinois, 1973.
  Occult Experimentation. Moody Press, Chicago, Illinois. 1972.

Christensen, Larry
  The Christian Family. Bethany Fellowship, Minneapolis, Minnesota.

Freeman, Dr. Hobart E.
  Angels of Light. Logos International Publishing Co., Plainfield, New Jersey, 1969.

Hagin, Kenneth
  Ministering to the Oppressed. P. O. Box 50126, Tulsa, Oklahoma, no date.

The Authority of the Believer. P. O. Box 50126, Tulsa, Oklahoma, no date.

Lindsey, Hal
Satan is Alive and Well on Planet Earth. Zondervan, Grand Rapids, Mich. 1972.

Macmillan, J. A.
The Authority of the Believer. Christian Publications, Inc., Harrisburg, Pa. no date.

Penn-Lewis, Jessie, and Roberts
War on the Saints. Christian Literature Crusade, Fort Washington, Pa. no date.

Whyte, Rev. H. A. Maxwell
The Power of the Blood. Whitaker Books, Monroville, Pa., 1972.

Dominion Over Demons. Whitaker Books, Monroeville, Pa., 1969.

Pulling Down Strongholds. Whitaker Books, Monroeville, Pa., 1971.

INSPIRATIONAL CATALOGUE AVAILABLE

If you have enjoyed this book you may want to read other publications that are available through Banner Publishing. We have listed books on the next pages that we feel will be of interest to you. Our catalogue describes these and hundreds of other inspirational Christian books and cassette tapes.

To receive a catalogue or order any of these books, send your name and address to:

------------------ DETACH HERE ------------------

Banner Publishing
504 Laurel Drive
Monroeville, Pennsylvania 15146

Please send me a copy of your catalog.

NAME_____

ADDRESS_____

_____ZIP_____

Suggested Inspirational Paperback Books

ACTS OF THE GREEN APPLES—Willans	$1.45
BAPTISM IN THE HOLY SPIRIT: COMMAND OR OPTION—Campbell	.95
CAN A CHRISTIAN HAVE A DEMON—Basham	1.25
CLIMB MOUNT MORIAH—Brooks	1.25
DEAR DAD, THIS IS TO ANNOUNCE MY DEATH—Kast	1.25
DOMINION OVER DEMONS—Whyte	.95
FACE UP WITH A MIRACLE—Basham	1.25
FAITH UNDER FIRE—Panos	.95
GATEWAY TO POWER—Smith	1.25
A HANDBOOK ON HOLY SPIRIT BAPTISM—Basham	1.00
A HANDBOOK ON TONGUES, INTERPRETATION AND PROPHECY—Basham	1.25
HE SPOKE—AND I WAS STRENGTHENED—Mills	1.25
HOLD ON TILL MORNING—Keller	1.25
IF I CAN, YOU CAN—Esses	2.25
THE LAST CHAPTER—Rasmussen	1.25
THE LAST JEW OF ROTTERDAM—Cassuto	1.25
LET GO!—Fenelon	.95
LET US MAKE MAN—Beall	1.25
LOOKING TO JESUS—Monod	.50
MINISTERING THE BAPTISM IN THE HOLY SPIRIT—Basham	1.25
THE NEW WINE IS BETTER—Thom	1.25
THE POWER OF THE BLOOD—Whyte	.95
THERE'S DYNAMITE IN PRAISE—Gossett	1.25
A SCRIPTURAL OUTLINE OF THE BAPTISM IN THE HOLY SPIRIT—Gillies	.50
SEVEN TIMES AROUND—McKee	1.25
SIMMER DOWN SAINT—Woerner	1.25
UNDERSTANDING GOD—Gruits	3.00
VISIONS BEYOND THE VEIL—Baker	.95
WHITE IS THE HARVEST—Jeffery	1.25